S0-ACU-898

*O*n *F*reedom's *F*rontier

The First Fifty Years of the
American Civil Liberties Union in Washington State

by Douglas Honig and Laura Brenner

American Civil Liberties Union of Washington
Seattle, 1987

Acknowledgements

Special thanks to the ACLU members who provided interviews and access to their personal papers, and to those who offered helpful criticism of the project. Thanks to Paul Dorpat for finding and obtaining photographs and to the *Seattle Times* and the *Seattle Post-Intelligencer* for the use of their photographs. Thanks to Polly Freeman, whose work as production administrator extended even into proofreading, and to Madeline Kesten and Nancy Osborne who typed, and retyped, the manuscript. Thanks to Rachel da Silva who designed the book, did the paste-up, and provided needed production assistance, and to Franklin Press for typesetting and production facilities.

Copyright © 1987 by American Civil Liberties Union of Washington
All rights reserved. No part of this book may be reproduced in any form without the written permission of the publisher, except for brief excerpts for the purpose of review.

ACLU
1720 Smith Tower
Seattle, WA 98104

ISBN: 0-9619283-0-1
Printed in U.S.A.
First edition
10   9   8   7   6   5   4   3   2   1

Library of Congress Cataloging-in-Publication Data

Honig, Doug, 1947-
    On freedom's frontier.

    Bibliography: p.
    1. Civil rights — Washington (State) — History.
2. American Civil Liberties Union of Washington — History.
I. Brenner, Laura, 1953-   II. American Civil Liberties Union of
Washington. III. Title.
KFW411.H66   1987   323.4′09797   87-19573

Table of Contents

On Freedom's Frontier

Introduction

This book traces the history of the Washington affiliate of the American Civil Liberties Union. For over five decades the ACLU-W has worked to safeguard the freedoms of citizens. At times, it has supported the political rights of activists striving to change society: labor organizers, Communists, civil rights workers, draft resisters, Indian rights advocates, women's liberationists. More often, it has upheld the personal freedoms of ordinary individuals in extraordinary situations: a Japanese American defying a Presidential internment order, a teenager made a ward of the court for driving 60 mph. in a 50-mph. zone, an Air Force nurse threatened with losing her job for having a baby, a student suspended from school for wearing slacks to class.

The mission of the civil liberties group is to protect individual rights, to limit the ability of government and other institutions to take away freedoms. The ACLU insists on enforcement of the guarantees of the Bill of Rights: the rights to free expression and association; the rights to due process and equal treatment by law; the rights to a fair trial and to protection from cruel and unusual punishment; the rights to privacy and to practice one's religion. Further, the ACLU treats the Constitution as a living, evolving document which must continually be applied to new situations.

Strategies and tactics for safeguarding rights have changed with the times. In its early years lawsuits and letters of protest were the ACLU's main tools. Later on, legislative lobbying and public education campaigns became just as important. On occasion civil libertarians have scored major gains just by the threat of lawsuits or even by losing legal cases which then raised public awareness of the need for reform.

For its work the ACLU has been called "annoying but indispensible" and has received praise for performing "outstanding

1

service to the cause of true freedom." It has also been castigated as "anti-God, "a Communist dupe," and "a lobbyist for porn." Such verbal blasts typically confuse civil liberties issues with the acts of people whose rights the group has defended. Indeed, it has aided the controversial and the eccentric, the notorious and the power-less. But it stands for freedoms, not causes. The ACLU has spoken up for the rights of people all across the political spectrum: for Senator Joseph McCarthy and for victims of McCarthyite witch hunts; for John Birch Society crusaders and anti-war protesters; for Police Guild members and targets of police surveillance; for the Moral Majority and for gay rights activists.

The development of the ACLU's Washington affiliate has been far from linear. It was founded amid the political ferment of the 1930s, went into wartime hibernation during the 1940s, revived in time to battle McCarthyism in the 1950s, expanded geometrically during the 1960s, weathered a life-threatening financial crisis dur-ing the 1970s, and attained new vitality during the 1980s. Over the years it evolved from a small, all-volunteer group centered around a board of directors in Seattle to a large, statewide organization with an active membership and a professional staff.

The evolution was not easy. Board members had to work out serious differences over the organization's identity. Some saw it primarily as a lawyer's group which must retain an aura of respect-ability to remain effective. Others saw the need for a large mem-bership base and a more activist stance. The key changes came in the 1960s, when the group for the first time opened its own office, hired full-time staff, and undertook fundraising to support a much-enlarged program. By the late 1970s the civil liberties agenda had broadened dramatically to include the rights of women, minor-ities, and those in institutions.

Whatever its size, the Washington group has often been in the forefront, on the frontier of civil liberties. The ACLU-W was among the first state affiliates to call the draft unconstitutional, to support Indian treaty fishing rights, to advocate the legalization of marijuana, to urge the impeachment of Richard Nixon, to oppose preparations for nuclear warfare — all as ways to protect individ-ual freedoms. And it served as a catalyst for coalitions which made Seattle the first American city to desegregate its public school system without a court order and the first to enact legislation curbing police spying on political activists.

The ACLU-W of the 1980s may seem far removed from the handful of people who 50 years ago — without their own office, telephone, or bank account — came together to further civil liberties in Washington. Today the organization has over 7,000 members, seven paid staff workers, and more than 400 cooperating attorneys and volunteers. Now computers organize a wealth of information for the group, mass mailings mobilize its members, staff and board coordinate a wide variety of projects, and regular fundraising campaigns support all the activities.

Yet the basic task, defending and extending constitutional rights, has not changed over the years. The story of the group bears out a vital lesson drawn by national ACLU founder Roger Baldwin: "No fight for civil liberties ever stays won." Issues have been fought and then refought. Efforts to censor books and stifle free speech persist. Zealots still try to preach religion in public schools. Computerized police intelligence files of political dissidents recall union blacklists and "subversive" lists of earlier eras.

The ACLU-W continues to face important struggles. Its challenge is to maintain the victories and adapt their precedents to changing conditions.

The Founding Years

A Spark of Outrage

The Great Depression of the 1930s brought both widespread hardship and political ferment to Washington. Thousands of workers were jobless, families lost their homes, and a Hooverville of tarpaper shacks arose on the tide flats near downtown Seattle. These conditions spawned a host of schemes and dreams for bettering society. Senior citizens rallied for old-age pensions. The unemployed demonstrated for relief programs. Those who had jobs formed unions and walked the picket lines. An alliance of left-wing groups called the Washington Commonwealth Federation became a major force in state politics. Postmaster General James Farley is said to have described the situation as, "The 47 states and the soviet of Washington."

Ed Henry was a Sociology student at the University of Washington in the early 1930s. Intensely concerned about poverty, he would go with friends down to Seattle's Skid Road and listen to speakers on soapboxes. On one corner he'd hear an economist advocating Communism. On the opposite corner would be a man pushing Socialism. Across the street someone would hold forth about Anarchism, and across from him would be a lady preaching Holy Roller Christianity. After the speeches the student and his buddies would drop in at the Pittsburgh Cafeteria (future site of the Brasserie Pittsbourg) at First and Yesler to discuss the problems of the day and ponder solutions.

Police on horseback sometimes dispersed the crowds with clubs and pulled speakers off their soapboxes in mid-sentence, claiming they had no right to speak without permits. Henry was outraged after witnessing one such roughhouse display in 1931. For help he contacted Carl Brannin, a political activist whom he knew from debates at the Seattle Labor College, a free community school. Brannin telephoned Roger Baldwin, head of the American Civil Liberties Union in New York. The civil liberties champion pointed out that the best way to combat such governmental abuses was to form a local ACLU group. Henry wrote for permission to do so, and the ACLU headquarters offered encouragement. Though the path would not be smooth, the groundwork was being laid for a permanent civil liberties organization.

Depression-era rally near Seattle's Pioneer Square.   *Seattle Times.*

Early Origins

The organization to which Ed Henry turned, the American Civil Liberties Union, was then but a decade old. It had come to life in response to repression of dissent and had committed itself to defending political freedoms.

America's entry in 1917 to World War I — touted as "the war to make the world safe for democracy" — brought intolerance for opponents of the fighting. Socialist Party leader Eugene Debs and labor organizer Big Bill Haywood were among hundreds of activists sent to prison; pacifists opposed to military service likewise were jailed. Victory in Europe did not end fears of subversion in

America. In 1919 and 1920, U.S. Attorney General A. Mitchell Palmer ordered raids on the offices of dozens of radical groups. In a campaign that would be known as "the Red Scare," Federal agents rounded up activists around the country, deported aliens, and seized tons of documents — all without evidence of any specific crime.

In this climate Roger Baldwin, a young social worker in St. Louis, in 1917 formed a civil liberties bureau within the American Union Against Militarism to aid conscientious objectors. More conservative AUAM members opposed assisting the war's critics, so the bureau soon became a separate agency. Baldwin himself served time in prison as an objector to military service. After the war, in 1920, Baldwin and associates in New York founded the American Civil Liberties Union as an independent organization. It took on the broader task of safeguarding the free speech and free assembly rights of all citizens. Baldwin would direct the Union for the next three decades. His passion for constitutional freedoms and dedication to the group's mission would prove crucial to its growth.

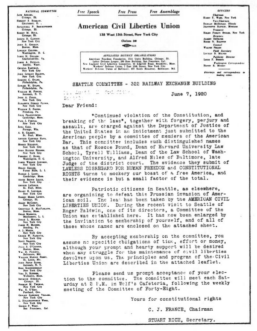

First membership recruitment letter for the Seattle Committee of the ACLU, 1920. Austin Griffiths Papers, University of Washington Historical Collections.

American Legionnaires commemorating "Centralia Massacre" clash with Wobblies.
Seattle Times.

In 1920 a small group of people also began meeting in Seattle to discuss civil liberties violations in Washington State. The area had been a hotbed of radical activism. The political establishment responded strongly here as elsewhere. During the war the Municipal League, a civic reform group, had ousted the Reverend Sydney Strong, pastor of the Queen Anne Congregational Church, for his pacifist views. Outraged citizens had recalled Anna Louise Strong, his daughter, from the Seattle School Board for supporting people arrested for opposition to the war. A vigilante group called the Minute Men had spied on fellow citizens it considered subversive. These self-appointed civic guardians claimed to have fostered over 10,000 investigations and 1,000 arrests in the first six months of 1918 alone.

Labor unrest fueled fears of radicalism. In 1919 Seattle's trade union movement staged the first general strike in an American city to support shipyard workers fighting wage cuts. Though the five-day action was totally nonviolent, civic leaders such as Mayor "Holy Ole" Hanson denounced the shutdown as an example of creeping Bolshevism.

The militant Industrial Workers of the World — better known as the Wobblies — had a regional headquarters in Seattle and organized strikes in the state's logging camps and lumber mills. Calling for "One Big Union of all workers," they met bitter resistance from public authorities and private interests. In a tragic conflict on Armistice Day of 1919, American Legionnaires attacked the Wobbly hall in Centralia. One Wobbly was lynched and seven received lengthy prison terms, but no Legionnaires were prosecuted for their role in the "Centralia Massacre." In its aftermath posses of armed Legionnaires scoured the countryside to round up Wobblies. Department of Justice officials seized the plant of the *Union Record*, the labor-backed newspaper in Seattle, and arrested staff members (including Anna Louise Strong).

The State Legislature gave legal teeth to the postwar Red Scare by passing a Criminal Syndicalism Law. In 1917 Governor Ernest Lister had vetoed a similar bill as a threat to the civil liberties of loyal citizens. But in 1919 broad, vague legislation was enacted that made it a crime to advocate, teach, publish, or further any doctrine promoting force as a way of bringing about social change. Eighty-six people were convicted under the law during its first year on the books.

The need for an organization to protect political rights was clear. Roger Baldwin visited Seattle in 1920, helping to establish a committee to form an ongoing civil liberties union. The first recruitment letter to organize a Washington branch went out on June 7, 1920 under the national ACLU letterhead:

> "Continued violation of the Constitution and breaking of laws, together with forgery, perjury, and assault are charged against the Department of Justice of the U.S . . . .
>
> "This lawless disregard for human freedom and constitutional rights turns to mockery our boast of a free America . . . .
>
> "By accepting membership on the committee, you as-

sume no specific obligations of time, effort, or money, although your prompt and hearty support will be desired when any struggle for the maintenance of civil liberties devolves upon us . . ."

The committee of about 20 met Saturday afternoons in Wolf's Cafeteria at 813 Second Avenue in downtown Seattle. Supporters generally had ties to the city's labor movement. The first chair was attorney Clemens J. France, the Farm-Labor Party candidate for U.S. Senate in 1920. Other members included George Vanderveer, an attorney whose defense of Wobblies and other outcasts would win him the sobriquet "counsel for the damned"; Carl Brannin, a Socialist and director of the Seattle Labor College; and pacifist minister Sydney Strong. Their goal was to recruit a hundred members.

It would be many years before this milestone was reached. The political turbulence which gave rise to the committee soon was over. The end of wartime production meant the loss of many jobs in Seattle's shipyards. Union membership plummeted, and conservative leaders won control of what remained of organized labor. With many activists in jail, the Wobblies lost much of their vitality. Prosecutions under the Criminal Syndicalism Law waned. As the

---

Religious Freedom: The Tremain Case

The first recorded case the ACLU handled in Washington involved a classic infringement of freedom of religion. In 1925, nine-year-old Russell Tremain of Bellingham refused to salute the flag in his public school class. A member of the Elijah Voice Society, he believed that saluting the flag was a warlike act contrary to his pacifist religion's teachings. When Russell's parents kept the boy out of school, authorities took him from home and put him up for adoption; a Juvenile Court judge backed the action. ACLU members interceded on the boy's behalf and helped work out a compromise with officials that would have allowed him to attend a private school. Though his parents rejected this proposal, authorities did eventually agree to drop the flag-saluting issue and allowed Russell Tremain to return to his parents.

national ACLU's 1927 annual report wryly noted, "The reason for the decrease in repression is that there is little to repress."

Although the initial Seattle ACLU committee never became a viable organization, individual members took the initiative to contact the national office for advice and funds for specific civil liberties cases. A leading concern was obtaining release of Wobblies jailed after the Centralia Massacre. Adele Parker-Bennett, a writer, worked for this through her Washington Conciliation Committee and received national ACLU money in 1928 to maintain a Seattle office.

She and Carl Brannin often did not see civil liberties issues eye-to-eye. The Socialist activist complained that Parker-Bennett had "a decided anti-communist complex and a violent twist for pussy-footing respectable procedure." For her part, the author observed that Brannin "just lacks tact." It was a difference of approach that would recur many times in the organization's history.

Wobblies imprisoned after "Centralia Massacre," including Ray Becker (front row, far right), last to be released in 1939. *Seattle Times.*

Revival

The upsurge of activism and repression brought by the Depression sparked another attempt to form a civil liberties group. In 1931, University of Washington student Ed Henry became the first executive secretary of the new Seattle ACLU Committee. Joining him in the group were three people who would be its mainstays for many years: attorney Irving Clark, future Democratic state senator Mary Farquharson, and the Reverend Fred Shorter, pastor of the Pilgrim Congregational Church. Free office space was provided in the Lyon Building near the courthouse by Marion Zioncheck, a young attorney who had recently masterminded the recall of Seattle's mayor.

Like its predecessor in the 1920s, the revived committee focused on securing political rights for unpopular activists. The Seattle ACLU aided aliens threatened with deportation and helped Communist-led groups obtain city permits for parades. Zioncheck won the acquittal of strikers arrested for unlawful assembly. Members objected to new loyalty oaths for teachers, backed a campaign to remove military training from the U.W. campus, and deplored beatings of Filipino farm workers in the Kent Valley.

Henry proved an energetic organizer. He set up a volunteer legal committee of prominent attorneys willing to assist in civil

---

Censorship: The Sex Book Case

In 1931 a customs inspector in Seattle seized as obscene a shipment of 120 copies of The Sexual Life in its Biological Significance by Dutch author Dr. Johannes Rutgers. The importer, C.E. Midgard, an impoverished advocate of sexual reform, sued to recover the books. The national office of the ACLU took the case, engaging Seattle attorney Frank Walters as counsel.

The trial drew newspaper headlines and titillated the Seattle populace. Before a crowded courtroom Walters delivered a dramatic defense of the value of the Dutch book, including an explicit account of the mechanics of sexual intercourse. An all-male jury ruled Midgard was entitled to regain possession of his goods.

liberties cases. He spent several hours in the office of Governor
Roland Hartley seeking pardons for the Centralia Wobblies. The
governor refused but did recommend paroles; all but one were
released.

The ACLU committee remained an informal operation; someone would hear of a problem and ring up other members to call a
meeting. Efforts to gain new members were strictly ad hoc. Ed
Henry relates that on one occasion they picked up a rather unlikely
recruit:

> "I was addressing a May Day celebration at Woodland
> Park on the right to free speech. A policeman interrupted
> to say that I couldn't talk without a permit, which I didn't
> have. A couple listeners suggested that we make the inci-
> dent a test case. So I insisted on continuing to speak, and
> the policeman arrested me and put me in his car.
>
> "On the way downtown he suggested we stop for a cup
> of coffee. Over coffee he asked, 'What's this group you
> belong to and how much does it cost to join? It sounds like a
> good outfit.' I told him we were the ACLU and membership
> cost two dollars a year. 'Here, I'll join,' he said. So he gave
> me his two bucks, I gave him a receipt, and then he started
> to leave.
>
> "'Wait a minute — you've got to put me in jail,' I
> reminded him. 'No, I'm all through,' he replied 'I per-
> formed my service — I stopped you from speaking.' And he
> just drove away. So we got a new member but couldn't have
> a test case."

The organization again slumped in 1933 when Zioncheck left
to take a seat in the U.S. Congress and Henry followed him to
Washington, D.C. to work in Congress and attend law school.
Meetings became infrequent. But civil liberties violations during
Seattle's bitter longshore strike of 1934 soon spurred local interest.
At the urging of the Reverend Raymond Atteberry of Grace Meth-
odist Church, a recent U.W. graduate named Paul Olson set about
organizing yet another committee.

Official Founding

June, 1935 marked the official birth of the Seattle branch of the American Civil Liberties Union. For the first time, both an executive secretary and an executive committee were elected. With its assortment of unionists, activists and intellectuals, the committee had the flavor of a New Deal coalition:

Paul Olson (executive secretary)
Chester Harman (chair) — Maritime Federation
Ed Weston — Secretary of the Metal Trades Council
Claire Vause — former official with state's
    National Recovery Act Compliance Board
Joseph Harrison — U.W. English professor
William Tucker — librarian
Joseph Jackson — secretary of the Seattle Urban League
Mary Farquharson — Democratic state senator
Fred Shorter — minister
Irving Clark — attorney

The group swung into action in defense of labor's organizing rights. An ACLU team investigated the use of the National Guard during a 1935 strike at Tacoma's lumber mills: "To say that the city is an armed camp of terror is not an exaggeration," reported Paul Olson. Attorneys Jack Cluck of Seattle and Frank Morgan of Hoquiam got injunctions barring the state patrol from interfering with peaceful picketing. During the hard-fought Newspaper Guild strike in 1936 against the *Seattle Post-Intelligencer*, the ACLU again acted to protect peaceful picketing and mass meetings.

The civil liberties group often found itself at the center of controversy. In 1936 police raided a Communist-sponsored Social Science School in Seattle, arresting a teacher and five students. Then a mob of World War I veterans burst in to break up a class and beat its students. The Seattle ACLU protested the attack and won release of the students. A headline in the *Post-Intelligencer* labelled the civil liberties advocates "Red Defenders."

Controversy did not cause the group to back off from supporting free speech and assembly. It defended the rights of students to pass out anti-war literature and persuaded the Seattle Park Board to designate three parks where meetings could be held without a permit. The ACLU sued the Bellevue School District for denying

ACLU stalwart Mary Farquharson speaking up for civil liberties at meeting in Bellevue. *Seattle Times.*

use of its buildings for meetings of the Washington Common-wealth Federation. Member Jack Cluck won the case by arguing that public buildings were meant for public use regardless of the popularity of the opinions espoused within their walls. To empha-size the point, the ACLU sponsored a protest rally in the Assembly Room of the King County Commissioners. In response to com-plaints by the Daughters of the American Revolution, the Ameri-can Legion, and the *Seattle Times*, the commissioners issued a statement declaring their facilities open to all public groups.

Two of the most successful campaigns completed work begun in the days of the Red Scare. For nearly 20 years the Criminal Syndicalism Law had provided the government with a handy tool for suppressing soapbox orators and dissident groups. The ACLU had begun lobbying to rescind it in 1933. Late in the 1937 legislative session, supporters of repeal led by State Senator Mary Farquhar-son maneuvered the bill out of committee. With the clock stopped to avoid ending the session and the bill the last measure of the day to be considered, the State Senate voted 34-10 to repeal the Criminal Syndicalism Law. Governor Clarence Martin signed the measure wiping the loathsome act off the books.

Two years later, after two decades of trying to budge a recalcitrant political system, Ray Becker, last of the incarcerated Centralia Wobblies, gained freedom from Walla Walla penitentiary. Work by ACLU members Mary Farquharson, Fred Shorter and Benjamin Kizer, a Spokane attorney, was instrumental in this release.

The case was a difficult one for politicians and civil libertarians alike. Believing he had done nothing wrong, the Wobbly — like many an ACLU client — would accept nothing less than complete vindication. He refused a pardon because it implied guilt and instead sought a hearing to correct factual errors from his original trial. "To such a move," he noted scornfully in one letter, "the national director of the so-called civil liberties union would be hostile." In his letters to the Seattle Chapter, Roger Baldwin urged the group to treat Becker with kid gloves lest he feel manipulated or cheated of his rights. Baldwin arranged a job for him through a wealthy benefactor who admired the Wobblies' courage. Finally, in 1939 Governor Martin commuted Becker's sentence on condition that he be escorted out of state by ACLU board members Fred Shorter and Mary Farquharson. The pair met him at the prison and drove him to meet friends in Oregon, thus ending one of the longest cases in state ACLU annals.

Communists and the 1940 Resolution

In defending various dissident groups, the ACLU had consciously taken on the mission of working for the rights of people with minority viewpoints. Yet many civil libertarians had misgivings about the presence of Communist Party members in their own ranks. The question of how to relate to Communists caused a major conflict, one that would trouble the civil liberties group for over two decades.

By the late 1930s the Communist Party of the U.S.A. had tens of thousands of members and was an important influence in many unions and political coalitions. Many Americans viewed the Party suspiciously, especially after the Hitler-Stalin Pact of 1939. Some ACLU'ers argued that no member of a secretive party could be a true civil libertarian. Others felt that associating with Communists undermined the group's credibility with the general public. Defenders of Communist members responded that discriminating against anyone for his or her political associations was inconsistent with civil liberties principles, that a denial of anyone's rights weakened the rights of all.

One telling incident involved Seattle attorney John Caughlan, who had joined the ACLU in 1936 soon after passing his bar exam. He describes the un-civil libertarian treatment given when he acted as legal counsel for the Communist Party:

"In 1937 the Communists had obtained a lease for use of the Civic Auditorium — the building that is now the Opera House — for a rally at which their leader Earl Browder would speak. John Dore, mayor at the time, swore that no goddamned Communists were going to meet in his civic auditorium and cancelled the lease. Morris Raport, the Party's district organizer, asked me to see what could be done. I said sure.

Academic Freedom: The Williamson Affair

In 1953 trustees of Eastern Washington College of Education granted unearned academic credit to the school's Director of Athletics. Professor Obed Williamson was one of several faculty members to file protests saying that the man had failed to complete work for their courses. All the protesting professors were dismissed without hearing or notice and subsequently were denied pensions.

While the other professors eventually left the college to find new positions, Williamson, aided by the ACLU-W, continued to press for a fair hearing. In 1958 a delegation from the ACLU-W approached Governor Albert Rosellini to urge that he appoint more fair-minded people to vacancies on the board of trustees. That was done, and a hearing was finally held. Williamson was reinstated and his pension rights restored.

"Well, I was relatively young and inexperienced and made some errors. I went back to my office to dictate the necessary material to show cause why the city should be found in breach of the contract. I gave it to the secretary and waited for the typed draft. Instead, I was summoned ·before the senior partner of the firm. He was holding the dictation as if it were contaminated and asked, 'Well, would you like to get out of the office right now? Or do you want to drop the case and stay till next Monday?' I left immediately — there didn't seem to be too much option.

"Anyway, I somehow managed to get the pleading filed in Superior Court. In the meantime, word had gotten out to the press. So upon leaving the court, I was greeted by the *Times*, *P-I*, and *Star*, who all wanted a statement. I commented very offhandedly that important civil liberties issues were involved and that it seemed natural for me to take the case since, after all, I was secretary of the ACLU.

"Whereupon, without my knowledge, the ACLU called a sort of rump meeting and read me out of the organization, terminating my secretaryship. You might say there was a slight absence of due process."

The national organization dealt with the issue of Communism by adopting the so-called "1940 Resolution," a contradiction to basic civil liberties principles. It stated, "The ACLU needs and welcomes the support of all those and only those whose devotion to civil liberties is not qualified by adherence to Communist, Fascist, KKK or other totalitarian doctrine." As a result, Elizabeth Gurley Flynn was ousted from the national board, and national chair Harry Ward was forced to resign.

The Seattle ACLU supported the resolution. For years the group would be ambivalent about taking actions that might associate it with Communists, though it did defend their right to a place on the ballot. The 1940 Resolution was repealed in 1967. John Caughlan was later personally invited to rejoin the ACLU of Washington by its executive director and served on its board in the 1960s. He had compiled a distinguished record in civil liberties cases, including successfully defending singer Paul Robeson when the city of Seattle tried to cancel a contract for him to sing in the Civic Auditorium.

Wartime Hibernation

By the late 1930s the Seattle ACLU organization had again fallen into disarray. Paul Olson had moved out of town, and board chair Irving Clark had resigned for health reasons. National director Roger Baldwin kept in touch by letter and was distressed to find the group faltering. "The Seattle committee has lain down on the job at a time when it ought to be increasingly active," he lamented in 1940. Mary Farquharson assumed responsibility for day-to-day business and was primary correspondent with the national office throughout the war years. "The Seattle chapter is coming on by jerks and starts," she reported in 1941. "I am acting as temporary chairman simply because there was no one else to do it . . . . However, we have taken on a number of new members — most of them have paid only $1, so we are keeping it for local expenses."

During the war the national ACLU remained active, aiding conscientious objectors and defending Jehovah's Witnesses whose children were expelled from school for refusing to salute the flag. The Seattle branch was essentially in hibernation. Individual members, however, did work to alleviate the plight of Japanese Americans suffering under the wartime internment program. And Mary Farquharson, Irving Clark and Ed Henry (now back in Seattle) all helped raise money for what some would call "the civil liberties case of the century."

Japanese American Internment

The bombing of Pearl Harbor outraged Americans, and U.S. entry to World War II stirred patriotic fervor. As wild rumors spread of a coming invasion of the Pacific Coast, "No Japs Wanted" signs began to appear. Though Japanese American civic groups declared their loyalty to the United States, President Franklin Roosevelt gave in to the wartime hysteria. In 1942 he signed an executive order directing that Japanese Americans be forcibly removed from the West Coast. One hundred and twelve thousand Japanese Americans — two-thirds of them U.S. citizens, over 13,000 of them Washington residents — were relocated to inland detention camps.

Nearly all affected Japanese Americans were forced to live in

Gordon Hirabayashi, whose conviction for violating World War II internment order was vacated in 1986. *Seattle Post-Intelligencer.*

the cramped, barbed wire-enclosed compounds. But Gordon Hira-bayashi, a University of Washington student and a Quaker, refused to register for internment or to comply with a curfew order. With Arthur Barnett (a future ACLU-W board member) as his attorney, he challenged the government actions in court as abridge-ments of his constitutional rights. Roger Baldwin provided ACLU money for the case. The U.S. Supreme Court in 1943 supported the government's policies as justified by military necessity, and the young Japanese American spent a total of nine months in jail.

Four decades later, Gordon Hirabayashi — by now a university professor in Canada — sought legal redress. With the help of a new generation of Japanese American activists, he sued for a writ of *coram nobis* to reverse his conviction because of fundamental errors in his trial. A hearing showed that the U.S. Department of War in 1943 had withheld information and made false allegations. A government attorney involved in the original case testified that the War Department had received numerous official reports from the FBI and the Navy that Japanese Americans posed no threat to national security. This information, proving the essential falsity of the charges, had not been disclosed to Hirabayashi in the original case. In 1986 U.S. District Court Judge Donald Voorhees vacated Hirabayashi's wartime conviction for violating the internment order.

Much had changed in the 40 years following the first trial. The passage of the Freedom of Information Act enabled Hirabayashi to obtain crucial documents explaining government policy. A Japanese American community willing to face squarely the pain of the past gave strong backing to the suit, raising over $60,000 for the cause. Attorneys donated over $300,000 in legal work. The ACLU of Washington, the American Friends Service Committee and other groups supported the case by helping with fundraising and providing legal assistance. Arthur Barnett, Hirabayashi's original attorney and longtime ACLU member, had the satisfaction of working on the legal team that won vindication.

The Cold War Era

Revival, Again

"Seattle Chapter of ACLU Revived Here Last Nite" proclaimed a headline in the *Seattle Times* of October, 1946. Soon a board of directors and a volunteer executive secretary were again functioning, and by 1948 Mary Farquharson could boast to Roger Baldwin that the group was "in the best shape it had been for a long time." Prime movers were attorneys, such as Max Nicolai, Solie Ringold, and Ken MacDonald, and University of Washington professors, such as Donald Wollett of the Law School. Meetings were now held in the University District at Fred Shorter's Church of the People. The outspoken minister had been ousted from Pilgrim Congregational Church in the 1930s for supporting social action causes; he and his followers had established a nondenominational church known for its Sunday free speech forums.

With its limited resources, the Seattle ACLU worked to uphold civil liberties by submitting *amicus curiae* (friend of the court) briefs in lawsuits initiated by others. The group backed local labor activists, including ACLU board members Nick Hughes and Ed Weston, in a longstanding battle for democratic control of their union. When members of Local 104 of the Brotherhood of Boilermakers had acted to cut officers' salaries, officials of the International Union had seized control of the local. Attorney Ed Henry, supported by an ACLU *amicus* brief by Mary Ellen Krug, won a decision from the State Supreme Court in 1949 saying the local had the right to run its own affairs.

The civil liberties group also came to the aid of Blacks living in Pasco, near the nuclear reservation at Hanford. It investigated charges that they were being denied jobs, accomodations, and city services. ACLU representatives met with city officials and David Lilienthal, head of the Atomic Energy Commission, to protest the discrimination.

Young civil libertarians picketing Canwell Committee hearings in Seattle, 1948.   *Seattle Times.*

McCarthyism

Just as the Red Scare had followed World War I, another wave of hysteria about radicals came on the heels of World War II. This time its sweep was broader, and it was known as "McCarthyism," after the Senator from Wisconsin elected in 1946 with the slogan

"Send a Tail-Gunner to Congress." He and his supporters portrayed American Communists as part of a conspiracy masterminded in Moscow that aimed at subverting our democratic system. With the U.S. locked in a Cold War with Russia, McCarthyism played on public insecurities about Soviet-backed regimes in Eastern Europe, Russia joining the U.S. in possessing the atom bomb, and Communists coming to power in China.

Joseph McCarthy was master of the big lie, the half-truth, and the unsubstantiated accusation. His tactics, followed by disciples in local communities around the country, were to smear liberal and leftist opponents as Communists, Communist sympathizers ("fellow travelers"), or dupes. The accuracy of the charge didn't really matter; in the paranoid atmosphere of the Cold War, mere allegation was enough to ruin a reputation. And people who defended the rights of Communists or alleged Communists were likely to have their own patriotism attacked.

Washington had its own precursor of McCarthyism. In 1947 the state legislature established the Joint Fact-Finding Committee on Un-American Activities, better known as the Canwell Committee for its chair Representative Albert F. Canwell, freshman Republican and former deputy sheriff from Spokane County. The seven-member body had a broad mandate to investigate individuals and groups that sought "to foment internal strife . . . to infiltrate and undermine the stability of our American institutions . . ." The committee held two sets of hearings in 1948 at the Field Artillery Armory (site of today's Seattle Center House). The first examined the Washington Pension Union, the second targeted the University of Washington.

The ACLU sought to restrain the Canwell Committee by proposing procedures to ensure due process rights. As board President Ivan Rutledge put it, "The purpose of the recommendations is to secure the essentials of fair play in the conduct of the hearings." At committee sessions, however, ACLU observers saw a complete flouting of fairness and due process. Testimony relied heavily on the opinion and hearsay of imported "expert" witnesses who had made a career of testifying against alleged Communists. Those accused had no right of defense or cross-examination, and their attorneys were not allowed to state objections. John Caughlan, defending one of the accused, asked if his client would be allowed to state objections.

> "No, he will not," said Canwell. "We are not going to debate the issue of the legality of this Committee or its procedures."
>
> "I have another question to ask," responded Caughlan.
>
> "You will ask no more questions," ordered the chairman. "We are not going to go on with any ridiculous procedure here. You will either comply with the instructions of this Committee, or you will be removed . . ."

Many who objected to the Committee's tactics were indeed forcibly ejected from the hearings.

In the wake of that witch hunt, three University of Washington professors were dismissed from their jobs, and the reputations of hundreds of other people were besmirched. So many people cancelled subscriptions to the Seattle Repertory Theater that owners Burt and Florence James, two Canwell targets, had to sell the theater. In 1949 and 1951 the State House and Senate passed bills creating committees similar to the former Canwell committee, but the proposals died in conference committee. The Spokane legislator himself lost a 1949 bid to move up to the State Senate and was defeated in several later bids for office. In 1955 Canwell admitted to the State Legislature that he had burned many of his committee's records. Yet he would be heard from again.

One Canwell victim successfully fought back. University of Washington philosophy professor and future ACLU board president Mel Rader convinced the King County Prosecutor to file perjury charges against star witness George Hewitt, who had accused Rader of being a supersecret Communist trained at a furtive Party school in New York. When officials tried to extradite Hewitt to stand trial in Washington, he was, ironically, defended by two civil liberties attorneys who had handled cases for the ACLU in New York. The Seattle ACLU branch rallied to Rader's aid, and board president John Richards of the University Law School wrote a strong letter supporting Rader's cause to the national ACLU staff counsel. Extradition was denied, but Rader presented irrefutable evidence of the perjury to University of Washington President Raymond Allen. Following a four-hour confrontation between Rader and Canwell in his office, Allen in 1949 issued a statement exonerating the professor. Reporter Edwin Guthman told the story in the *Seattle Times* under banner headlines, winning a Pulitzer Prize for his coverage. Rader chronicled the 15-month battle to clear his name in *False Witness* (University of Washington Press, 1969).

McCarthyism remained a potent force. Nationally ACLU thinking was arrayed along a spectrum from support of the Cold War to defense of the rights of Communists. In Seattle the group was wary of taking actions which would have even the appearance

University of Washington professor Mel Rader (right) conferring with attorney Ed Henry at Canwell Committee hearings, 1948.   *Seattle Times.*

of associating it with Communists. In 1954, for example, the board struggled over the question of whether to sponsor the appearance of Harvey O'Connor. A longtime political activist and former Seattlite, O'Connor had pleaded First Amendment rights in refusing to tell the House Un-American Activities Committee (HUAC) whether he belonged to the Communist Party. Would sponsoring such a speaker taint the ACLU and hamper its effectiveness? Or was it the ACLU's role to provide public forums for controversial civil liberties figures? After lengthy debate, the board agreed to sponsor O'Connor — but with a public qualifier that it didn't necessarily endorse his views. (He later cancelled due to scheduling conflicts.)

On another occasion, the organization was split when Frank Krasnowsky, an avowed Trotskyite, sought to join. Members resigned — some in support of the man, others because they felt he had no business being a member under the 1940 Resolution. Ultimately, his membership was accepted.

Yet the ACLU did take many strong stands in defense of the rights of victims of McCarthyism. In 1954 the group aided Margaret Schuddakopf, a Tacoma school counselor fired for pleading the Fifth Amendment before HUAC. Faced with petitions signed by 20,000 people calling for her removal, Fred Haley, Tacoma School Board member and future ACLU board member, took out a large ad in a Tacoma paper to remind citizens of the importance of the Fifth Amendment. The School Board voted to retain Schuddakopf, but the Pierce County School Superintendent moved to fire her.

Washington State Superintendent Pearl Wanamaker ultimately upheld the Board's decision, making Tacoma one of the few school systems to continue employing someone who had defied HUAC.

In 1954 the House Un-American Activities Committee, then chaired by Harold Velde, paid Seattle a visit to probe alleged Communist activities in the Pacific Northwest. The ACLU, represented by Ken MacDonald, and other community organizations met with Velde to insist on due process and fairness. ACLU observers monitored the hearings, and ACLU members such as Benjamin Asia, Jack Harlow, and Phil Burton independently served as counsel for people subpoenaed before HUAC. When HUAC returned to Seattle in 1956, its guilt-by-association tactics were sufficiently discred-

ACLU-W mainstay Ken MacDonald (left) defending Communists on trial in Seattle, 1953.   *Seattle Times.*

ited that the Seattle-King County Bar Association agreed to provide attorneys for its targets.

In battling McCarthyism, the ACLU's concern was to protect rights to free speech and association, rights which the group advocated even for the demagogue himself. When the senator from Wisconsin stopped in Seattle during the 1952 election, officials of KING Broadcasting asked for an advance copy of his scheduled television address. KING refused to carry the speech, saying it contained potentially libelous accusations. The senator threatened to have the Federal Communications Commission revoke the station's license, and the Seattle ACLU wrote a letter protesting the curtailment of McCarthy's right to speak. FCC officials investigated the incident and ultimately ruled that KING had not acted improperly.

The U.S. Senate censured Joseph McCarthy in 1954. He drifted from the limelight and died in obscurity three years later. But the Cold War tensions which bred him and the chilling effects of his investigations would linger for years.

Cold War on Campus

Universities, as supposed bastions of free inquiry, were often battlegrounds over curtailments of civil liberties in the Cold War era.

A furor erupted in 1955 when U.W. President Henry Schmitz revoked an invitation to J. Robert Oppenheimer to deliver the annual Walker-Ames Lectures. The famous physicist had his security clearance revoked by the Atomic Energy Commission in 1954 because of his association with suspected Communists and his opposition to the development of the H-Bomb. Anxious about his institution's public image, Schmitz explained that "bringing him (Oppenheimer) here at this time would not be in the best interests of the University." Faculty members protested, and ACLU member Fran Hoague recalls a meeting of the University's Tenure Committee at which the president rushed into his office and announced that he was being hanged in effigy by disapproving students.

In a scathing letter to the *Seattle Times* the ACLU's Ken MacDonald called upon the Legislature to withhold funds from the University "until this act of fear and this assault upon free inquiry

---

Teachers' Rights: The Richard Jones Case

In 1960 an American U-2 spy plane was shot down over Russia just before a scheduled summit conference. After a class discussion, students of East Bremerton High social studies teacher Richard Jones sent President Eisenhower a telegram urging an apology to Nikita Krushchev for the violation of Soviet airspace. School officials in Bremerton, site of a major naval base, charged Jones with incompetence and relieved him of his teaching duties.

The ACLU-W wrote a letter to the School Board supporting Jones. "Refusal to subscribe to and propagate current political orthodoxy is not a symptom of incompetence," it declared. After the School Board upheld Jones's firing in a dramatic public hearing, the civil liberties group backed a lawsuit for the teacher handled by ACLU board member Ken MacDonald. In 1962 Judge Charles T. Wright of the Thurston County Superior Court ordered Jones reinstated to his teaching position.

and scholarship by Dr. Henry Schmitz be reversed." The university chapter of the ACLU co-sponsored a public forum to discuss issues surrounding the dispute. Although Schmitz didn't change his mind, the ACLU had made its point forcefully.

The ACLU's increasingly strong stance in defense of political activists partly reflected the arrival of younger new board members. People such as Reverend Aron Gilmartin, political scientist Alex Gottfried, psychologist Art Kobler, and attorney Leonard Schroeter worked strenuously to move the organization to a more activist role. One of Gottfried's first acts on the board was to gather all significant facts concerning University of Washington loyalty oaths and urge litigation.

Loyalty oaths were an insidious yet commonplace feature of life during the Cold War years. People in numerous occupations were required, as a condition of employment, to sign broad statements swearing that they had never been affiliated with "subversive" organizations. From 1947 until 1956, 42 states and over 2,000 local jurisdictions required such affidavits of loyalty from public employees. Washington had adopted a law in 1931 requiring teachers to swear to promote respect for governmental institutions. In 1951 the Legislature enacted a loyalty oath requirement for all public employees. Four years later it adopted as a test of loyalty membership in any group on the U.S. Attorney General's list of "subversive organizations," a blacklist of groups "suspected" of being subversive. Civil libertarians argued that having to vow that one wasn't "subversive" stifled academic freedom and promoted conformity of thought.

In 1955 the Washington ACLU mounted a legal challenge to the University's practice of requiring loyalty oaths and to its reliance on the U.S. Attorney General's list as the test of loyalty. ACLU attorneys Byron Coney, Fran Hoague, and Solie Ringold argued the oath requirement violated the First, Fifth, and Fourteenth Amendments. In an atmosphere charged with redbaiting, the ACLU took as plaintiffs Howard Nostrand, chair of the Romance Languages Department, and Max Savelle, an American History scholar, tenured professors with high national reputations.

The lawsuit followed a twisting path through the legal system. The ACLU won a Superior Court ruling that the loyalty oath was unconstitutional on technical grounds. The State Supreme Court, however, held only that portion of the statute involving the Attorney General's list was invalid. The U.S. Supreme Court remanded it to the state court on a new issue: whether employees were entitled to a hearing to explain a refusal to take the oath. The state court ruled that while employees in general had no right to a hearing, tenured professors did. In 1962 the Supreme Court refused to rule further, effectively ending the case; it was a victory for the two professors, but a ruling that didn't go far enough to suit the ACLU.

Another chance to challenge the loyalty oath soon arose. The U.W. Board of Regents issued a directive that the oaths be signed. By now the U.W. chapter of the American Association of University Professors was so aroused that it worked with the ACLU on another suit. The new legal challenge involved over 60 faculty and staff as plaintiffs and occasioned much bitter wrangling over legal strategy and who should serve as counsel. Ultimately ACLU attorneys Ken MacDonald and Arval Morris (also a U.W. law professor) argued *Baggett v. Bullitt*, the third test of the University loyalty oaths to reach the U.S. Supreme Court.

This time, in 1964, the high court overturned both the 1931 and 1955 loyalty oaths for being unconstitutionally vague, giving too much discretion to officials enforcing them, and depriving employees of due process. Though the ACLU had hoped for a decision on grounds that the oaths violated freedom of speech and association, the nine-year saga nevertheless ended in a major victory. After the Supreme Court decision, similar oaths in several other states were declared unconstitutional. In 1975, in a case brought for the ACLU by John Darrah, the State Supreme Court would invalidate the loyalty oath for candidates for public office — the last of Washington's loyalty oaths.

Organizational Growth

Under the threat of McCarthyism the Seattle-based ACLU grew from a couple dozen members after the war to 250 by the early 1950s. While a Tacoma ACLU chapter had existed briefly in the 1930s, activities had generally centered around King County. In 1952 the group changed its name from "Seattle Chapter" to "State of Washington Chapter" of the ACLU, reflecting a desire to broaden its reach. Later in the decade a statewide Advisory Committee of prominent individuals was established to further this goal. In 1958 the state chapter incorporated as the "ACLU of Washington, Inc." (ACLU-W), also known as the Washington affiliate.

Efforts to form chapters took place in Yakima, Spokane, and Tacoma. The latter got an unexpected boost from a Tacoma newspaper which had printed a letter to the editor claiming the ACLU was a Communist organization which "defends violence and preaches atheism" — the kind of charges the group would hear many times through the years. When ACLU leaders objected, the Tacoma paper printed a retraction, gave front-page play to an ACLU reply, and ran an editorial favorable to the civil liberties group.

As its membership grew, the organization began taking steps to become more democratic and enhance its ability to tackle more issues. Traditionally the Board of Directors had done nearly all the group's work. Board members such as Solie Ringold and Bob Brooks argued that since lawsuits were the ACLU's main weapons, it of necessity operated through a small core of people; they worried that involving the general membership would produce an unwieldy decision-making process. But others such as Len Schroeter and Aron Gilmartin pointed out that a strong base of public support was essential. So in 1954 new bylaws were enacted which replaced the old self-perpetuating board with one elected at a general membership meeting. (Voting by mail was approved two years later.) The monthly newsletter, another innovation, advised members to come early to the Friends Meeting House in the University District for the local ACLU's first election in 20 years. "Because it is the first time, we don't know how many to plan for, and the Homemade Pies will be served on a first come, first served basis," it cautioned.

With the job of voluntary secretary becoming increasingly time-consuming, the chapter voted to establish it as a part-time position paid the princely sum of $100 a month. R. Boland (Bob) Brooks served as executive secretary from 1953 to 1958. A Columbia University-trained lawyer, he had gone to prison as a conscientious objector during World War II; for this he was refused admission to the Washington State bar. Brooks gave the ACLU use of his personal telephone and of his home as office.

His work provided the organization with the stability it needed to handle more cases and keep both members and the press informed of its doings. From 1953 to 1956 chapter membership zoomed from 250 to 650; this paralleled the growth of the national ACLU, whose membership tripled from 10,000 to 30,000 during 1950-1955. Washington's finances remained precarious, however. The 1954 budget of $2,500 was balanced by the expedient of not paying the executive secretary for four months.

To involve members further, the group established a system of six organizational committees, plus five for subject areas: academic freedom, censorship, civil rights, due process, and free speech. Committees studied issues and problems and formulated recommendations to the board for action. Beginning in the late 1950s, the chapter sponsored a series of neighborhood meetings in Seattle-area homes of members; these get-togethers offered a chance to discuss civil liberties issues as well as to meet fellow ACLU'ers. The ACLU also began emphasizing member and public education more. It staged an all-day conference on the Bill of Rights, with separate workshops for its Articles. The event was the first of its kind for the Washington ACLU and it proved a rousing success.

Censorship, Church-State and Civil Rights

Nationally, the ACLU's work in the 1950s focused on issues which some have termed "the Four C's": Cold War, Church-State, Civil Rights, and Censorship. While Cold War-related problems generated the most impassioned debates, the Washington chapter was also active in the other areas. For example, the ACLU's Paul Detels and Don Davidson filed an *amicus* brief in a suit charging the state's statute regulating comic books was unconstitutional because it required vendors to furnish state officials with copies of all issues before sale and was so vague that no publisher could be sure whether he or she were violating it. In 1958, in *Adams v. Hinkle*, the State Supreme Court tossed out the law.

Attempts to censor literature and films would be an ongoing concern. The ACLU-W participated in a challenge to Seattle ordinances empowering a Board of Theater Supervisors to preview

Members of the Congress on Racial Equality demand end to racial discrimination in housing in Seattle, 1964.   *Seattle Post-Intelligencer.*

films for moral content and to punish theater owners with imprisonment and loss of license for movies deemed obscene. In 1965 in *Fine Arts Guild v. Seattle,* James Mifflin invalidated the laws as a prior restraint on freedom of expression. The State Supreme Court upheld the decision three years later.

Safeguarding the separation of church and state was a major

concern for civil libertarians. With its expanded geographic presence, the Washington ACLU became involved in a Spokane case about a practice called "released time." With the approval of school officials, the Spokane Council of Churches passed out cards which, when signed by parents, excused students from class to receive noncredit religious instruction at nearby churches. Spokane attorney Carl Maxey challenged the practice in court, backed by an ACLU *amicus* brief by Len Schroeter and Donald Voorhees. The civil libertarians lost. In 1959 the State Supreme Court, in *Perry v. School District No. 81*, upheld the religious program's validity, though the Court did object to the use of public schools for handing out consent cards.

In other instances, the ACLU gained favorable outcomes. In 1956, King County Jail inmate W.H. Rhea sued the Sheriff and 18 religious groups to bar them from holding religious services in the jail's corridors and "tanks." The ACLU's Ken Cox and Ken MacDonald filed an *amicus* brief arguing that since Rhea was truly a captive audience, the forced attendance at a worship service violated his constitutional rights. A judge refused to grant an injunction, but in the meantime the Sheriff issued a new rule limiting religious services to the chapel and a few empty tanks, thus making attendance voluntary. At the University of Washington, board member and professor Alex Gottfried led protests against a school-sponsored Religious Emphasis Week that used the student union and dorms for religious discussions. The events were banned in 1957 after the State Attorney General declared them unconstitutional. And in 1961, after several years of objections by the ACLU-W, the Attorney General delivered another ruling barring the distribution of Bibles in public schools by the Gideon Bible Society. Despite these rulings, many other forms of religious activities in public schools would pose continuing problems for civil libertarians.

The movement to end racial inequality increasingly became America's leading social justice crusade. Inspired by daring boycotts, sit-ins, and freedom rides, several ACLU-W members went to the South in the early 1960s to help on legal projects to protect civil rights activists. The work could be risky; Len Schroeter, for example, tells of being chased by a carload of state troopers late one night on a rural highway in Mississippi.

Back in Washington, the ACLU-W fought against the extradition of a Black man living in Spokane who was threatened with execution from a conviction in Georgia. Civil libertarians argued that Charles Will Cauthen had been denied due process because his murder trial had lasted only 30 minutes, with the jury deliberating a mere 10 minutes before convicting him. In 1964 Governor Albert Rosellini announced that he would not hand over Cauthen to Georgia officials.

The role of the ACLU-W was largely to provide legal and moral support to fights led by civil rights groups such as the National Association for the Advancement of Colored People, the Urban League, and the Congress on Racial Equality. The affiliate supported legislation which in 1957 made Washington the second state to ban racial discrimination in private housing transactions involving government insurance. In 1963 opponents of discrimination in housing staged sit-ins in the Seattle Mayor's and City Council offices. The ACLU-W lobbied for a "fair-housing" ordinance adopted by the Seattle City Council later that year. It was soon overturned by a referendum vote, but another open housing proposal the civil liberties group backed became Seattle law in 1968.

Religious Freedom: The Case of God's Little Candles

In September, 1962, Seattle police arrested members of God's Little Candles for soliciting funds without a license. The unconventional religious group believed that the United States was threatened by a Negro-Zionist conspiracy headed by Richard Nixon.

Though wary of the ACLU-W, the sect did allow executive director John Darrah to defend its right to the free exercise of religion. Darrah argued that the city's solicitation ordinance was overly broad and allowed too much discretion to public officials in granting licenses. A trial judge voided the ordinance, and a Superior Court judge upheld the decision in 1963. God's Little Candles resumed battling "the conspiracy" though with new reservations about fitting the ACLU into it.

In the courtroom the ACLU-W backed major lawsuits for an interracial couple seeking child custody and a Black buyer trying to purchase a house; unfortunately both lost on appeal. However, in a case supported by an ACLU-W *amicus* brief, the State Supreme Court in 1959 upheld an award of damages to Ola Browning, a Black woman in Seattle who had been denied service by a Slenderella salon.

Due Process

With Earl Warren as Chief Justice of the U.S. Supreme Court, the nation's judiciary delivered key decisions upholding the constitutional rights of citizens facing criminal charges. The ACLU-W was involved in several major cases supporting the right to due process. *State v. Murphy* concerned an accused murderer who had been given tranquilizers by the jailer before appearing on the stand. As a result, he testified mechanically and without showing remorse; he was convicted and given the maximum sentence. In 1960 the State Supreme Court ordered a new trial for Murphy, accepting the ACLU's contention (in an *amicus* brief by William Dwyer, Ralph Johnson, Len Schroeter, and David Skellenger) that Murphy had been denied a fair trial the first time.

In *State v. Cory*, the Washington Supreme Court in 1963 reversed a criminal conviction based in part on evidence obtained when deputy sheriffs bugged the attorneys' room in the Bremerton jail and eavesdropped on conversations between Cory and his lawyer. An ACLU *amicus* brief, submitted by Ken MacDonald, Marjorie Rombauer, and Maurice Sutton, argued that the whole trial had been tainted by this violation of the Sixth Amendment guarantee of effective representation by counsel.

Two other ACLU-W cases reached the U.S. Supreme Court. Spokane police had arrested Raymond Haynes for robbery and told him that he would not be permitted to see his wife or lawyer until he signed a confession. Fran Hoague, William Dwyer, and David Skellenger prepared ACLU briefs which pointed out that since Haynes's confession had been involuntary, it should be inadmissible as evidence under the due process clause of the Fourteenth Amendment. In 1963 the U.S. Supreme Court reversed Haynes's conviction.

Sixteen-year-old Robert Miller had been arrested for car theft in the late 1950s. A few days after his booking, police, without telling Miller, met with a juvenile court judge who agreed to waive jurisdiction so he could be tried as an adult. Miller ended up with a 10-year sentence. After several years in the penitentiary, on the advice of fellow prisoners, he filed a petition for *habeas corpus* arguing that under the Fourteenth Amendment he should have been granted a hearing with counsel on the waiving of jurisdiction. The ACLU-W provided assistance in further appeals. The U.S. Supreme Court ruled that Miller had been denied procedural fairness and remanded the case to Washington courts. In 1966 he won his release.

Rise of the Far Right

Joseph McCarthy had been disgraced in the mid-1950s, and a brief thaw in U.S.-Soviet relations ensued. At the beginning of a new decade there was much in the political climate to stoke the paranoia of right-wing extremists. The Cold War had not been won, and nearby Cuba was run by Communists. Black activists staged militant protests while the Supreme Court under Earl Warren's leadership imposed restraints on police. Liberal Democrats led by John F. Kennedy took power in Washington, D.C., and they openly approved of the civil rights movement and the fiscal "evil" of unbalanced budgets.

Thus, in the early 1960s a new far right movement arose. Like McCarthyism, it viewed the world in black-and-white terms and was intolerant of dissent. Adherents saw America as menaced by sinister conspiratorial forces in the garb of Democrats and occasionally Republicans; indeed, John Birch Society founder Robert Welch once termed the conservative Dwight Eisenhower "a dedicated and conscious agent of the communist conspiracy." The Birch Society was the largest of several organizations on the far right. This new extremist movement never gained the broad public support enjoyed by McCarthyism or the Red Scare, but it was strong enough to pose many problems for defenders of civil liberties.

The liberal Supreme Court was a *bete noire* of the John Birch

Society and its allies, for whom "Impeach Earl Warren" was a rallying cry. However, conflicts more often took place outside the courtroom. For example, the far right proposed that public schools add to their curricula so-called "American Heritage" programs aimed at instilling unquestioning patriotism. Civil libertarians such as Alex Gottfried, Arval Morris, and Mel Rader actively opposed such proposals, convincing school officials that it was their constitutional responsibility to promote free inquiry and critical thinking, not indoctrination.

A major battle with the far right took place over the distribution of two films in the public schools. *Operation Abolition* presented a distorted picture of 1960 demonstrations against the House Un-American Committee, showing protesters as Communists or dupes and HUAC itself as a fearless crusader against subversion. *Communism on the Map,* produced by Harding College in Arkansas, depicted Communism as a red tide washing across the globe and implied that Presidents Roosevelt, Truman, and Eisenhower were complicit in the spread of the menace. Besides public schools, the Boeing Company, holder of billions of dollars in defense contracts, showed the latter film both to its employees and numerous public groups. The ACLU-W countered with a statewide campaign of corrective literature and speakers. Members such as Giovanni Costigan and Art Kobler explained the films' distortions to audiences and urged that schools not rely on simplistic propaganda in teaching about Communism.

True to its principles, the ACLU-W defended the First Amendment rights of the John Birch Society, whose views the ACLU found obnoxious. When the Seattle Park Board refused the Birchers permission to hold meetings in the parks, the civil liberties group objected and convinced the Park Board to issue regulations ending political restrictions on the use of its facilities.

Nevertheless, far right groups attacked the ACLU as subversive. In the 1964 Seattle City Council race, ACLU members Jim Kimbrough and Robert Block made strong showings in the primaries but lost the general election after being branded pro-Communist and anti-God for their ACLU ties. Observed the weekly newspaper *The Argus,* "(ACLU are) initials which for some reason seem to inflame a certain variety of supercitizen these days like banderillas stuck in a bull." Similar attacks in eastern Washington led to a landmark courtroom showdown involving an ACLU member, an old foe, and the civil liberties organization itself.

The Goldmark Case

In 1962 John Goldmark, an Okanogan County rancher and three-term state representative, ran for reelection to the Legislature. The Democrat found himself the target of an elaborate smear campaign orchestrated by John Birch Society members, *Tonasket Tribune* editor Ashley Holden, and Albert Canwell, who had been chairman of the Legislature's Committee on Un-American Activities in the late 1940s. The *Tribune* termed Goldmark "a tool of a monstrous conspiracy to remake America into a totalitarian state."

John and Sally Goldmark relaxing on their Okanogan County ranch after filing suit against people who smeared them, 1962. *Seattle Times.*

A principal piece of evidence was the legislator's membership on the Washington State Advisory Board of the ACLU. Canwell, who had resurfaced as a free-lance investigator of subversive activities, described the ACLU as "the major Communist front operating in the state of Washington." And in an American Legion meeting at Omak, Herbert Philbrick, famous ex-counterspy, delivered a colorful assault on the civil liberties group as "not just red, but dirty red." The barrage was effective. The incumbent legislator lost the Democratic primary by a 3-1 margin.

Two weeks after the general election, John Goldmark sued Canwell, Holden, and two other defendants for libel. Representing the plaintiff were R.E. Mansfield of Okanogan and William Dwyer of Seattle.

The case would involve proving that Goldmark and his wife Sally weren't Communists and that the ACLU was not a Communist front group. A sidelight to the case involved a request by the plaintiff that the ACLU's membership list be released to aid in preparing the case.

The request caused a difficult test of principle. On the one hand, Goldmark was a staunch advocate of civil liberties smeared by people hostile to freedom of expression. And the trial would present a public showcase that could clarify to the general citizenry just what the ACLU stood for. The organization's policy from the very beginning, however, had been to respect the privacy of its members and never to disclose its roster of names. Were the list to fall into the wrong hands or be made public as evidence, individual members might suffer harassment. Board member Mel Rader argued that, to the contrary, his own experience before the Canwell Committee had shown him the value of community support as well as the danger of secrecy; members would better be served by open solidarity with Goldmark than by anonymity. At first the ACLU-W board voted to release the names. But on a later vote, following a three-hour discussion, the board decided 15-10 to withhold the general membership list, though it did agree that the names of the board members could be made public at the trial.

The courtroom drama lasted 10 weeks. Several ACLU-W board members testified, as did John Pemberton, executive director of the national ACLU. In explaining the group's philosophy and its belief in the First Amendment, Pemberton noted, "The ACLU has faith in the common man to think and choose." In January, 1964, an Okanogan County jury found the defendants guilty of libel and awarded the Goldmarks $40,000 in damages. Later that year the U.S. Supreme Court, in *Sullivan v. New York Times*, ruled that a public official or candidate for office cannot be considered libelled unless a statement was made with "actual malice" — knowledge that it was false or reckless disregard for its falsity: an *amicus* brief by the national ACLU had argued for this position. In response, Judge Theodore Turner set aside the jury verdict in the Goldmark case because nothing in the trial record proved the defendants had acted with "actual malice." Yet, the fact stood that both the Goldmarks and the ACLU had succeeded in clearing their names. Judge Turner noted that the verdict established that Goldmark "was not a communist nor a pro-communist"; that the ACLU "was not a communist front organization"; and that the defendants "made false charges."

The Warrant, Please: The See Case

In 1963 Seattle businessman Norman See was convicted of a misdemeanor in Municipal Court for refusing to let City Fire Department officials inspect his locked warehouse for possible fire code violations. See claimed that the Bill of Rights protected him against inspection without a search warrant. Officials presented neither a warrant nor any evidence of hazardous conditions in See's warehouse. However, the existing City fire ordinance authorized the fire chief to enter any building as often as he deemed necessary. The ACLU-W entered the case at the State Supreme Court level. Cooperating attorney Paul Jackson filed an amicus brief arguing that the fire ordinance violated the Fourth Amendment's protection against arbitrary searches. After losing at the state court, See appealed to the U.S. Supreme Court, where national ACLU legal director Melvin Wulf and New York University law professor Norman Dorsen joined Paul Jackson in presenting the ACLU's arguments. In 1967, in a decision by Justice Byron White, the U.S. Supreme Court ruled that Seattle's fire ordinance allowed an unconstitutional invasion of privacy without a warrant and tossed out See's conviction.

This case was the first court test in the United States of the "communist front" charge against the American Civil Liberties Union, and the organization was completely vindicated. William Dwyer wrote a moving account of the Goldmarks' story in *The Goldmark Case: An American Libel Trial* (University of Washington Press, 1984).

Expansion and Protest

A Model for Growth

Historically the ACLU had not been broadly based. The leaders of the Washington affiliate had mostly been lawyers, academics, and a few ministers, all centered around Seattle. In the mid-1950s the group had taken initial steps to become a membership organization — instituting an elected board, establishing the committee system, organizing a few chapters outside King County. Now, a decade later, some board members insisted that to be effective the organization needed to broaden its base of support and become more aggressive. However, proposals for changing traditional operations met objections. Could the group really do major fundraising? Wouldn't renting its own office end up swamping the affiliate with work? And how would it handle a flood of crank calls?

Under the leadership of board members such as Len Schroeter, who served as president in 1963 and 1964, the ACLU-W put aside its qualms and moved to expand. The affiliate undertook a vigorous membership recruitment campaign, taking over responsibility for membership services from the national office. The group established vastly higher budget goals and pursued fundraising drives to meet them. The risk-taking strategy proved a smashing success, and soon Washington could boast of the fastest growing affiliate in the country. In 1965 statewide membership approached 2,500, nearly triple what it had been at the start of the 1960s. The budget for that year topped $30,000, a tenfold leap from that of a decade before.

The ACLU-W expanded to become a truly statewide organization, including chapters in Yakima, Spokane, Pullman, Tacoma, Whatcom County, and Kitsap County that would become fixtures in the organization. Through the work of Rick Hull, who energetically filled the newly created position of chapter coordinator, the number of chapters would grow to 20 by 1970. Unfortunately, quite a few were sparked by short-term local issues and withered away after Hull returned to grad school to pursue his PhD. in English.

In the early 1960s the affiliate office in Seattle had little connection with happenings in eastern Washington. Members of the Pullman chapter were so frustrated by the difficulty of getting advice from Seattle that they seriously discussed seceding from the ACLU-W. But during the decade much greater attention was paid to involving out-of-Seattle members and providing services to chapters. In one key change, the Board of Directors was enlarged to include voting representatives from each chapter.

The civil liberties group also acted to make its operations more professional. In 1961 the ACLU-W for the first time rented its own office, on the 18th floor of the historic Smith Tower; a year later it moved up to the 21st floor, which would serve as headquarters for the next two decades. Longtime member Mary Gallwey recalls that the decor was far from posh:

> "I'll never forget the first time I walked into the office. The walls were pale, institutional green, with paint flaking and chipped. Utility pipes snaked through the rooms with valves the size of small dinner plates. Smaller pipes connected up with tilting sinks in the corners of most of the rooms. The furniture lacked legs of equal length, and you could sink down among the broken springs and come up with stuffing stuck to your clothes. I was astounded that people could get the organization's work done."

But work they did, including the first full-time paid staff. In 1964 Dave Guren, a district director of the California Democratic Council, was hired as the ACLU-W's full-time executive director. Margaret Wherrette served as office manager, and a year later Mike Rosen, a young attorney who had been doing civil rights work in Mississippi, became the first staff counsel. The addition of paid staff significantly changed the role of the organization. As Rosen explains, "Having a staff attorney meant that we could often provide direct representation to people. If you needed help, here was a live body standing beside you in the courtroom instead of an attorney arguing abstract theory for an *amicus* brief. This made the ACLU much more visible and credible in the community."

The national ACLU restructured, too. It had been controlled by an elite group of big city lawyers and intellectuals on the East

Coast. Roger Baldwin had envisioned local branches as satellites of the New York office, rather than as autonomous bodies. But as state affiliates became increasingly independent, they pushed for more say in the organization. At the watershed 1964 biennial ACLU national conference in Boulder, Colorado, the group adopted a federal structure that ended the self-perpetuating national board centered around New York and gave representation to state affiliates. Washington's Len Schroeter became the second person from west of the Mississippi to serve on the national body, and ACLU-W board member Art Kobler would later become the first Northwesterner elected to an at-large position.

The ACLU-W was a leader in this "Great Decentralization." As Len Schroeter recalls, "People at Boulder were amazed to hear of what we, a smaller state, had accomplished." The growth-oriented policies of the Washington, Michigan, and Southern California affiliates served as models for future development. The national organization adopted a record $1 million budget for 1965 and set out to organize new affiliates and chapters around the country, especially in the South. For six years Schroeter chaired the steering committee of the National Development Council, which oversaw the expansion program. The effort succeeded; from 1964 to 1969 the ACLU more than doubled the number of its affiliates. The new structure fundamentally altered the character of the ACLU. For behind organizational changes were differing notions of how the ACLU should approach its mission. Pragmatists, or "imagists," as some have called them, gave more weight to the public perception

Right to Privacy: The Paulsen Case

In 1963 the superintendent of Federal Way School District asked one of his janitors how he had voted in the last school bond election. "None of your damn business," snapped back the employee, Henry Paulsen. For his audacity with a superior, the janitor was fired.

The ACLU came to the defense of Paulsen's right to keep his job while keeping his voting record to himself. A judge ordered him reinstated. Paulsen had already secured another job, but he did receive compensation for lost wages — and no small measure of satisfaction.

of the group and were wary of taking actions that would alienate potential supporters. Risk-takers, or "activists," put a premium on making strong stands regardless of who might be alienated. The structural changes of the 1960s brought activists such as Len Schroeter to the fore. This, he recalls, meant a major shift in the organization's tone: "Our style was very different and therefore controversial. We were willing to make waves and say things that might seem disrespectful of the Establishment. We supported opening an office in the ghetto, representing Black Panthers, and providing direct legal counseling to draft resisters without worrying about how it might affect our image. Even our advocacy of paid staff and major fundraising caused a stir because it meant we were no longer a polite volunteer organization."

The Washington affiliate developed a reputation as a feisty group. Board meetings featured pointed arguments over principle and policy. "Some people saw the board as the best debating society they had ever experienced," recalled former ACLU-W board president Aron Gilmartin. "I would go to meetings just to hear the discussions. They were sharp. People didn't always agree, but the interchange was always alive." Others compared entering board meetings to walking into a lion's den. "Civil libertarians tend to be prickly people," explained Mary Gallwey, another board president. "They're very sensitive to incursions on their prerogatives and to feeling manipulated." Sometimes differences of opinion led to angry personal attacks or people stomping out of the meeting room. At one point, decorum at board meetings became such a problem that it was referred to the executive committee for consideration. Formally identifying insensitive behavior as a concern helped defuse some of the tension.

As a group, the ACLU-W was not afraid to stand up to the national office when it felt aggrieved, especially in financial matters. As Fran Hoague put it, "We didn't like to feel pushed or kicked around." Dues collected locally were banked in New York, and later the Washington affiliate would receive a percentage allocation. In 1957 the Washington branch had formally severed financial ties with national by keeping all the funds it solicited. This strong action came after the national office repeatedly altered the state's share of income; Washington leaders were especially peeved when they felt national had reneged on an agreement. The move to financial independence proved an administrative nightmare, as people had to take out separate memberships in both the state and national organizations. After a year the Washington affiliate reintegrated its finances with national.

The ACLU-W had continued to work with the national office on issues. In the 1960s the Washington group became known for pioneering policies. It was among the first affiliates to chart new courses on the draft, marijuana, Native Americans, and (in the 1970s) Presidential impeachment.

Exploding Tensions, Expanding Dockets

In 1968 two Black students were suspended from Seattle's Franklin High School for a fight they claimed had never happened. They sought help from members of the Black Student Union at the University of Washington, who arranged a meeting with Franklin's principal. Over 50 students trooped into his office, talked for a while, and remained there after he left. When a further meeting was arranged for the auditorium, the students left the principal's office. It was announced that the suspensions would be arbitrated by the City Human Rights Commission, and the students ended their demonstration.

The next week seven of the protesters were arrested for having participated in the sit-in. The two who were juveniles were handcuffed while in their school building. Bail was set at $1,500 each, but ACLU-W attorneys secured their release on personal recognizance. A defense team of staff counsel Chris Young, Gary Gayton, Ronald Meltzer, and Andrew Young represented Aaron Dixon, Larry Gossett, and Carl Miller in Justice Court, where they were convicted of unlawful assembly. On appeal King County Superior Court Judge Solie Ringold overturned the statute because it made criminal an individual's mere presence at an assembly which became disruptive. The State Supreme Court reversed the decision, but agreed that "mere presence" was insufficient to sustain a conviction. When the case was remanded to the lower court, the City declined to prosecute again.

Such supercharged conflicts were commonplace in the late 1960s and early 1970s. It was a hectic, free-wheeling era when the

authority of many institutions was under attack. Students boy-
cotted classes and marched down I-5 to protest the war in Vietnam. Young men burned their draft cards to defy military
conscription. Street people rioted in the University District, and
Blacks battled police in the Central Area. Members of the counter-
culture shocked middle-class society by wearing outlandish clothes
and advocating free love. Activists staged sit-ins, hippies sponsored
be-ins, and "potheads" held smoke-outs.

Challenges to established values and powers inevitably raised
civil liberties issues. Chris Young, who served as staff counsel
during 1968-1970, recalls that the ACLU-W was often in the thick
of the action:

> "The ACLU office was a real center of activity. Anyone
> with a question about their rights — students, hippies,
> people off the street — would come to see us. A lot had
> legitimate questions, though we also saw many flakes. In
> those days young people especially didn't know much about
> their rights, and here was a place to get information. The
> phones rang constantly. We'd get calls from tearful G.I.'s
> about to be put on the plane for Vietnam. It was incredibly
> intense.
>
> "There were all sorts of little confrontations — people
> with long hair pulled over by the police, street people
> busted for loitering just because they'd been hanging out on
> corners. Young protesters felt a real sense of urgency, that
> they had to do *something*. And political conditions were so
> polarized that abuses were extreme. I knew people who
> were beaten up in alleys by off-duty police after leaving
> anti-war rallies.
>
> "I'm sure the office felt alien to some longtime members.
> There would be youthful freaks all over. We were full of
> self-righteous zeal and had a save-the-world mentality.
> Everything established was thrown open to reassessment.
> Looking back, I know the intensity took its toll."

Indeed, one staffer tells of receiving crank calls, threatening
calls, even calls seemingly designed to set him up for prosecution.
He left his job with the ACLU-W convinced that his home phone
was tapped by the government.

From protests to fests, the ACLU-W was on the scene in the late 1960s.   *Russ Nobles and Cherry Severson.*

The ACLU-W had a presence in many arenas of conflict. In 1967 alone, the group was deluged with 9,000 requests for legal assistance. For a time in the mid-1960s it functioned as a de facto legal aid office since it was the only agency in the state with a full-time paid attorney to whom people could turn for free, sympathetic advice. Similarly, the Smith Tower headquarters was a popular source of advice on criminal cases before a public defender's office was established in Seattle in 1969, with former ACLU-W executive director John Darrah as the city's first Public Defender.

Traditionally the ACLU-W had focused its limited legal resources on filing *amicus* briefs in appeals of cases initiated by others. But with full-time staff, increased membership, and a larger budget, the civil liberties group could get involved in a much greater number and variety of cases. A growing cadre of idealistic young lawyers was willing to volunteer services as cooperating attorneys on specific cases, and the group made good use of law student interns and office workers provided by government social programs. As a result, the ACLU-W's docket expanded from seven cases in 1965 to over a hundred in 1971. New clients such as Black Panthers, Hare Krishnas, and leaders of the Seattle Liberation Front made significant contributions to the ACLU-W's record of defending civil liberties.

Freedom of Expression

As in earlier eras, public authorities sometime responded to social turmoil by trying to repress free speech. In a highly publicized case of 1967, Timothy Leary sought to present his "tune in,

---

Freedom of Association: The Robel and Schneider Cases

Eugene Robel had been a machinist at Todd's Shipyard in Seattle for over 10 years. In 1963 he was arrested under Section 5 of the federal McCarran Internal Security Act, which barred members of the Communist Party from working in defense plants. He faced five years in jail and a $10,000 fine.

The ACLU regarded the arrest as an example of guilt by association, for it penalized Robel for mere membership in the Party without alleging that he had committed any other unlawful act. Attorney John Sullivan filed the ACLU-W's amicus brief in the case, pointing out that the McCarran Act violated the First Amendment's protection of freedom of political association. In 1968 the U.S. Supreme Court voided Section 5 of the Act and tossed out the charges against Robel.

Herb Schneider, a Seattle marine engineer, had been denied seaman's papers for three years for refusing to answer questions by the Coast Guard concerning his political beliefs and associations. ACLU-W board members Len Schroeter, John Caughlan, and Chas Talbot represented Schneider in a legal challenge to the Magnuson Waterfront Screening Act, which called for the questioning. In 1968 the U.S. Supreme Court ruled 8-0 that such screening infringed on the First Amendment rights of free speech and association.

Stokeley Carmichael at Seattle's Garfield High after the ACLU-W obtained a court order enabling him to speak there, 1967. *Seattle Times.*

turn on, drop out" philosophy at the Seattle Opera House. Responding to a petition circulated by irate PTA mothers, the Seattle City Council refused to rent the building for what Leary billed as a "Psychedelic Religious Experience." The ACLU supported Leary in a legal challenge, but the State Supreme Court upheld the City's power to deny him the use of public property. The apostle of mind expansion through drugs ended up renting a private hall and drew a large crowd swelled by all the controversy.

In the same year, the ACLU-W did win the right for another controversial figure to speak in a public building. The Seattle School Board refused to rent Garfield High School's auditorium for an address by fiery Black activist Stokeley Carmichael out of fear his appearance would inflame racial tensions. Attorney Ray Brown handled Carmichael's lawsuit for the ACLU. Judge Frank James of the King County Superior Court, in *Carmichael v. Bottomly*, ruled that the School Board had failed to show valid grounds for barring the activist's speech in a building open to public use.

Sometimes freedom of expression involved symbolic forms of protest, such as altering the American flag. In 1970 Harold Spence of Seattle protested the U.S. invasion of Cambodia and the killing of four students at Kent State University by displaying in his apartment window a flag with a peace symbol taped upon it. He was arrested, convicted of "misuse of the flag," and sentenced to 30 days in jail. ACLU-W cooperating attorney Peter Greenfield argued that Spence's act was free speech protected by the First Amendment. The Superior Court upheld Spence's conviction, the Court of Appeals overturned it, and the State Supreme Court reinstated it. Finally, in 1974, the U.S. Supreme Court ruled that the statute had been unconstitutionally applied to Spence since he had engaged in an act of free speech. *State v. Spence* was the first flag desecration case decided directly on First Amendment considerations.

The ACLU-W also defended the right of an individual to burn the flag as another form of symbolic, if unpopular, free speech. As Maxwell Morris, president of the Kitsap chapter, put it, "The flag is only a symbol of government, and burning it does no more to destroy that government than erasing a word does to destroy the English language." The battle ended when the State Supreme Court, in *State v. Turner* (handled for the ACLU-W by Phil Burton), reversed the conviction of a man who had burned the Stars and Stripes at a rally in Seattle in 1967.

Civil libertarians extended the notion of symbolic free speech to include the right of individuals to express their own lifestyle. In 1969 Seattle City Light threatened to fire male employees who worked in trenches 10-15 feet below the ground for having long hair or sideburns below the middle of the ear. The official justification of this policy was the need to maintain a good public image. Mike Rosen (by that time ACLU-W executive director) informed a *Seattle Times* reporter, and the paper published a story with a cartoon which depicted citizens peering into a manhole and expressing shock at the sewer workers' long sideburns. City Light quickly dropped the threat. Some ACLU members complained that such haircut cases were frivolous and a waste of staff time. Rosen replied that government control over personal habits was highly offensive, and the right to wear one's hair as he or she pleased was a basic freedom of expression issue.

"Straight society" was often horrified by the way the counter-culture and young people flouted traditional standards of behavior. As a result, hippies and youths could suffer harassment for seemingly petty actions, and the ACLU was called on for help. For example, in 1968 Michael Brunson, 19, was selecting a flower for his shirt lapel from a dumpster outside a flower shop in Seattle's University District. Two policemen looking for people throwing illegal drugs in trash bins arrested the youth for "tampering with garbage cans." The ACLU got the charges dismissed in this and many similar cases.

One of the most controversial lifestyle issues was marijuana. In an extreme overreaction, a judge imposed a 40-year sentence for a man who had sold one "joint" to a minor. The ACLU-W's Arthur Barnett filed an *amicus* brief arguing the sentence was unconstitutionally cruel and unusual punishment. In *State v. Williams* the State Supreme Court in 1970 reversed the man's conviction.

The ACLU-W was one of the first affiliates to assert an individ-

---

The Right to Counsel: The DuPuis Case

In 1964 Norbert DuPuis, a Native American living in eastern Washington, was charged with carnal knowledge. Having been stabbed in the chest three days before his arraignment, he was scarcely in any condition to comprehend his legal rights. He told the judge that he had no memory of the alleged crime but that since a deputy sheriff said he had committed the act, he "guessed" he'd plead guilty. After failing to appoint an attorney, the judge accepted the guilty plea and sentenced DuPuis to life in prison.

ACLU-W staff counsel Mike Rosen filed a petition of habeas corpus, arguing that DuPuis had not intelligently waived his right to counsel. In 1966 the State Supreme Court in DuPuis v. Maxwell accepted the petition and ordered DuPuis released from prison.

ual's right to use marijuana as a matter of privacy. It argued that use of pot was a victimless crime involving voluntary action by an adult. The group mobilized national effort to testify before the Legislature in an unsuccessful effort to liberalize state marijuana laws. The ACLU-W also worked with the coalition BLOSSOM (Basic Liberation of Smokers and Sympathizers of Marijuana), sponsor of a 1974 initiative to legalize possession of small amounts of marijuana in Seattle; not unexpectedly, it lost 2-1. But Seattle did adopt a new law replacing most criminal penalties for marijuana possession with civil fines.

Protest

One morning in the late 1960s, eight college students were handing out leaflets about the draft on the edge of the grounds of Bellingham's Sehome High School. They were arrested for violating the state vagrancy statute which prohibited loitering "without a lawful purpose" outside of a school. ACLU-W defense attorneys Rand Jack and Eugene Eugster argued that the distribution of literature was indeed a "lawful purpose," one protected by the First Amendment.

"I remember saying, 'What a great case to take to the U.S. Supreme Court,'" recalled former ACLU-W Legal Counsel Mike Rosen. "But we'd have to lose at Justice Court, Superior Court, and the State Supreme Court first, and there seemed no way that could happen." But "the impossible" happened. At a Whatcom County Justice Court trial protected by armed sheriffs fearing violence, the students were convicted and sentenced to five days in jail. The Superior Court and the Washington State Supreme Court upheld the decision. Given the chance to rule on *State v. Oyen*, the U.S. Supreme Court in 1972 threw out the conviction.

In the late 1960s and early 1970s the ACLU-W took on many cases which sought to safeguard the First Amendment rights to freedom of speech and assembly for dissenters. Civil libertarians recognized that people who broke the law could not expect to escape punishment because of the rightness of their cause. But they challenged the application of some laws and the constitutionality of others when used to stifle dissent.

The war in Vietnam, which ultimately brought the death of
over a million Vietnamese soldiers, another million South Vietnamese civilians, and 58,000 American soldiers, was the leading
cause of dissent. The early anti-war protests of the mid-1960s were
usually peaceful. In 1965 the Reverend Harold Bass contracted
with the City of Tacoma to place 20 signs on buses saying "End War
in Vietnam Now by Peaceful Negotiations — Urge Use of Resources for Peace." After receiving complaints that the placards
were "traitorous," "anti-U.S.," and "peacenik," the city manager
ordered their removal. The ACLU-W sued the city, and Judge
Horace Geer of Pierce County Superior Court, in *Hillside Community Church v. City of Tacoma*, ruled that the First Amendment forbade
the City from censoring political ads on buses; the State Supreme
Court upheld the decision.

Meanwhile, students from Western Washington University
were staging an orderly procession along Bellingham sidewalks
with signs urging negotiations and withdrawal from Vietnam.
Police arrested them for failing to comply with an ordinance requiring 24-hour notice of a parade in the street. Fredric Tausend
argued for the ACLU-W that the protesters had been denied equal

Sitting down on Seattle's Fifth Avenue to protest the Vietnam War, 1972.   *Seattle Times.*

protection of the law because a sidewalk procession was not covered by the street parade ordinance. The judge agreed, acquitting two students and dismissing charges against 38 others.

As the war dragged on and U.S. involvement in the bloodshed escalated, protests grew more strident and more frequently included acts of violence. After demonstrators broke windows at a tumultuous February, 1970 rally at the U.S. Courthouse in Seattle, seven anti-war activists were charged with conspiracy to destroy Federal property. The ACLU-W assisted in the defense of Jeff Dowd and Roger Lippmann, two of the group who became known as "the Seattle Seven." The Washington affiliate helped cover costs for a four-person defense team of Lee Holly, Michael Tigar, Jeff Steinborn, and Carl Maxey.

It was a highly controversial decision taken only after much heated debate. Opponents of ACLU involvement argued that the defendants might try to turn the trial into a political forum rather than a defense of constitutional freedoms. Some worried that members who disapproved of the radical protesters would cease supporting the ACLU-W. Still others objected that the board was interested in the case for its publicity value. However, advocates of ACLU participation pointed out that the case involved a basic civil liberties issue — the use of vague conspiracy laws which essentially punished the "crime" of thought. The evidence indicated that the seven hadn't conspired to anything; as Dowd put it, "We can't even agree on the time of day." The defendants were not charged with having committed any of the rally's property destruction. Rather, the overt criminal acts cited in the indictment included studying maps, making a speech, leading a march, and taking karate lessons. In May the ACLU-W Board of Directors voted 19-2 to take the case, a decision reaffirmed by a narrow 16-13 margin a month later.

The trial itself, held in Tacoma, revealed that the prosecution's case relied heavily on the dubious testimony of a police informer who had infiltrated the Seattle Liberation Front, a network of political collectives. The proceedings ended in a mistrial, with Federal Court Judge George Boldt (better known for a later decision on Indian treaty rights) summarily citing the defendants for contempt of court; they had refused his summons to come to trial one morning in protest of the exclusion of some supporters from the

courtroom. The ACLU-W presented an *amicus* brief to the Ninth
Circuit Court of Appeals, which reversed the contempt citations
because they were issued without a hearing and contained too
general a description of the defendants' actions. In a rehearing the
Seattle Seven, by now weary of their acrimonious legal battle,
pleaded *nolo contendre* (no contest) and were sentenced to various
terms for contempt. In 1973 the U.S. Attorney dropped the conspiracy charges. In the aftermath of a 1970 bombing at the U.S. Capitol, a Federal grand jury was empaneled to investigate anti-war
activism. A chief target was Leslie Bacon, a young woman who
herself was not known to have committed any unlawful acts but
who had associated with movement leaders back East. Federal
authorities located the grand jury in Seattle because they viewed it
as a receptive jurisdiction and hoped that by isolating Bacon from
friends and supporters, they would lead her to implicate others.
Things didn't work out quite as planned.

The ACLU-W, viewing the grand jury as essentially a "fishing
expedition" for information about anti-war protesters, represented
Bacon. When she refused to answer more than the first few questions, the government granted her "use immunity," meaning that
she must testify or be jailed, though her testimony could not be
used against her directly. Bacon refused and was found in contempt of court; the judge denied ACLU attorney Jan Peterson's
move to have the complaint quashed unless the government re-

The Right to Be Wrong: The Elks Case

*In 1966 the Richland School District rented one of its buildings for one
night to the Elks Club. The Congress on Racial Equality brought suit to
enjoin the meeting because the Elks were racially segregated. Although the local
ACLU chapter opposed a long-term lease for another discriminatory group, in
this instance it felt that the Elks' First Amendment rights to hold a meeting took
precedence. The civil liberties group filed an* amicus *brief supporting the
Elks, and the court agreed.*

*The ACLU attorneys then joined members of CORE in picketing the
Elks meeting. As one of the lawyers explained, "I believe in the Elks' right to be
wrong in a public place — and in my right to tell them that they are wrong."*

ACLU'ers Bob Free (left) and Norman Siegal seeking court order to end bombing of Cambodia from Justice William O. Douglas in Goose Prairie, WA, 1973.   *Oregon Journal.*

vealed evidence obtained from wiretapping. The Ninth Circuit Court of Appeals upheld the contempt citation but granted a stay until the issue could be decided by the U.S. Supreme Court. Federal authorities had miscalculated Bacon's toughness and the ability of the local protest community to mobilize support. Faced by her steadfast refusal to implicate other activists, the government released her.

Late in the war, an ACLU-W staffer was involved in a dramatic sidelight to the conflict. In 1973 the New York affiliate had sued the Federal government to halt the bombing of Cambodia. The East Coast group appealed an unfavorable decision to the U.S. Supreme Court, which was out of session, and sought help from the Washington affiliate in tracking down Justice William O. Douglas for a hearing. Legal intern Bob Free happened to answer the phone when the call for assistance came and thus became the one to accompany New York lawyer Norman Siegal in a search for the renowned jurist at his retreat in Goose Prairie. Free relates the adventure:

"I was scared to death. I felt like I had the weight of the world on my shoulders. Justice Douglas didn't have a phone, and I didn't even know where Goose Prairie was. How were we going to find his house — with no address on an unmarked road — in the dark? What if we got there when he was still asleep? Do you wake up a Justice?

"Well, after we finally found the house, we waited outside till morning. Douglas had the reputation of being very brusque, and I was expecting to get a dressing down for disturbing his peace. At last he came out and talked to us and was actually very pleasant. Douglas said, 'Give me an hour to review the papers and come back.' He decided to hear oral arguments the next morning."

But Douglas's order to stop the bombing immediately was overruled by Justice Marshall after he discussed the case with the other justices over the telephone. Douglas was highly critical of Marshall, as it was extremely unusual to overrule a decision based on a phone conversation. The case got tied up in procedure until it became moot. The wave of protest subsided as the U.S. withdrew its troops and signed a peace agreement with North Vietnam in 1973.

The Draft

The Vietnam War prompted reconsideration of longstanding policies on military service. Historically the national ACLU had held that although such service deprives citizens of basic individual liberties, this could be justified for national defense or in time of emergency. Thus, the ACLU had not opposed the draft during World War II or the Korean War, but had stood against universal military training in peacetime. In 1966 the ACLU-W board split evenly over competing approaches to the issue. Half favored one of two traditional approaches — either that the ACLU should limit its concern to the appropriateness of the government's draft program or that it should determine whether world political conditions warranted a draft. The other half, led by Alex Gottfried and Art Kobler, backed a major departure — that conscription so thoroughly violates civil liberties it should be opposed in every instance. A year later, the ACLU-W became one of the first affiliates to adopt a resolution supporting the latter position, namely that the draft should be opposed as a form of involuntary servitude violating the Thirteenth Amendment. (ACLU policy is generally the same nationwide, but the organization's motto is "unity, not uniformity." Thus, affiliates from time to time take differing positions.) In 1972 the Ninth Circuit Court of Appeals rejected a direct legal challenge to the draft's constitutionality by ACLU-W cooperating attorney Bill Hanson.

The Washington affiliate also began to support the right of an individual to obtain conscientious objector status for objecting to a specific war. To give concrete assistance the ACLU-W established the Seattle Lawyers Draft Panel, a draft counseling project which aimed to enable individuals to use their legal rights to follow their conscience.

The government at times targeted people critical of the draft. In 1967 John Peffers of Seattle and Jeffrey Hess of Tacoma learned the hard way. They were ordered to report for induction to the military after handing out anti-war leaflets at draft physicals. The

---

Juvenile Rights: The Lesperance Case

In 1967 Laurel Lesperance, 17, received a citation for driving 60 mph in a 50-mph zone. A traffic referee suspended her license for six months and turned down her parents' request that she be allowed to drive two hours a day to help out with the family store. Her parents appealed to Juvenile Court. Though the girl had never before been to Juvenile Court and had never even received a prior traffic ticket, the judge affirmed the license suspension.

A week after the hearing, Laurel's parents received a court order declaring their daughter "a delinquent child in danger of growing up to lead an idle, dissolute, or immoral life" and making her a ward of the court till age 21. The ACLU-W's Ross Runkel and Mike Rosen appealed to the State Supreme Court. The Court reversed the Juvenile Court's decision, noting that the girl had not been informed of her right to counsel and pointing out the deficiency of a juvenile statute which makes any minor who breaks any law "a delinquent."

ACLU sued, charging the two were being punished for their political activities. A week before their trial Selective Service officials
withdrew the induction order, and the U.S. Attorney assured the
ACLU that future protesters wouldn't face such harassment.

Beyond the Courtroom

Some ACLU-W members were uncomfortable with the group's
relation to the controversial protest movements of the era. They
complained that in aiding militant anti-war protesters, defiant
Black Panthers, and rebellious youth, the organization had departed from defending against encroachments on civil liberties to
serving simply as legal counsel for "the movement." Executive
Director Mike Rosen responded that the traditional approach of
protecting freedoms by selecting test cases wasn't always relevant
to pressing issues. "Waiting for repression to occur and then trying
to fight it is often an exercise in futility," he argued. "To create a
climate favorable to civil liberties we must commit ourselves to a
broad attack on inequities."

Civil libertarians with an activist approach have insisted that
the ACLU-W had a duty to look beyond narrow interpretations of
constitutional rights. "We use the Bill of Rights as a starting point,
but civil liberties go farther," longtime board member Alex Gottfried has said. "Some ACLU people imagine the last belch of the
Supreme Court defines individual freedom. But that puts us in an
awkward position when we have a Supreme Court that is anti-civil
libertarian. We have nowhere to go if we allow government to tell us
what civil liberties are." According to a report in the *Seattle Times*,
the ACLU won 80 percent of its cases that reached the U.S. Supreme Court during the 15 years (1953-1969) of Chief Justice Earl
Warren's leadership. The figure dropped to around 50 percent
during the early 1970s.

ACLU strategy had long relied primarily on setting legal precedents through test cases. While litigation remained a vital tool,
public pressure and legislation became increasingly important. As
ACLU-W board president Al Ziontz explained at a quarterly
meeting in 1966, "We have traditionally fought for these (civil
liberties) values by invoking the holy writ of the Constitution and

asking the men in black robes to interpose its doctrine against the masses. However, in the long run the ACLU must be able to operate effectively outside of the legal arena."

To be sure, the ACLU-W had often spoken up for or against the passage of certain laws and had employed part-time lobbyists. However, in 1973 the group decided to make lobbying a priority and hired Michelle Pailthorp as its first full-time Legislative Director, a position she held for five-and-a-half years. Often joining forces with Legal Services attorneys, she became an effective operator in the rough-and-tumble maneuvering of legislative battles. In her 1975 annual report Pailthorp noted that the ACLU-W's status in Olympia had changed dramatically. At first, she related, the mere mention of an ACLU endorsement could be the "kiss of death" for a bill. But now even conservative legislators were paying attention to critiques by the civil liberties group. "One lobbyist ignored an ACLU-W proposal with a disdainful 'What can they do?'" reported Pailthorp. "He found his bill rerouted to another committee, where ACLU language was tacked on by a conservative Republican deeply concerned with privacy rights." Legislators were even asking to sponsor ACLU proposals. Among its major victories the civil liberties group counted the 1976 reform of the Juvenile Code providing that the state no longer had the right to incarcerate "incorrigible children" who had never committed a crime.

The ACLU-W had periodically sponsored speakers on civil liberties issues and concerns. Larger-scale efforts at educating the public and mobilizing support on specific problems also took on greater importance. A classic example targeted a longtime nemesis of civil libertarians, Richard Nixon. As an ambitious young California politician in the late 1940s, he had won seats in the U.S. House and then the Senate in part by redbaiting his liberal opponents. Indeed, his use of McCarthyite tactics had won him the slippery nickname of "Tricky Dick." Two decades later, as President, he secretly ordered the bombing of Cambodia, supervised burglaries of political opponents, and attempted to cover up details of the ensuing Watergate scandal. In mid-1973 the national ACLU took the unprecedented step of calling for the impeachment of the President for subverting the Constitution; it was the first national organization to make such a call.

Members of the Washington affiliate were initially divided over undertaking an impeachment campaign because it was so obviously a political action. But as ACLU'ers wrestled with the issue at an affiliate conference in Ellensburg, word of Nixon's notorious "Saturday Night Massacre" of Cabinet officials filtered in. Board members and chapter leaders huddled around a rickety TV set to get the news. Next morning they agreed to plunge into the campaign. It was the ACLU-W's most ambitious project yet, involving petitions, letters to Congress, phone calls, and a series of public forums around the state with speakers such as Giovanni Costigan. Thousands of citizens attended a teach-in at the University of Washington co-sponsored by the ACLU-W and featuring historian Henry Steele Commager, liberal senator Fred Harris, and

---

Academic Freedom: The Wagle Case

Lawrence Wagle, a history teacher at R.A. Long High School in Longview, became chair of the new southwest Washington chapter of the ACLU-W in the mid-1960s and twice served on the state affiliate's Board of Directors. The teacher ran afoul of school authorities after he began taking controversial stands: Wagle challenged the tradition of holding religious baccalaureate services on school property as a violation of church-state separation; he wrote a letter to a newspaper supporting the ACLU position in favor of legalizing marijuana; he distributed a pamphlet comparing the student-teacher relationship to a form of slavery.

In 1970 officials declined to renew his contract, saying he was an incompetent teacher. Wagle sued to regain his job, charging he had been fired for his ACLU activities. ACLU member Fred Noland represented him. When a trial jury accepted Wagle's contention and ordered him rehired, the judge overruled the verdict as not warranted by the evidence. The Ninth Circuit Court of Appeals reversed the judge's action, finding that the jury's decision had been reasonable. In 1977 the U.S. Supreme Court ordered the appellate court to reconsider its ruling in light of revised judicial standards. Lawrence Wagle's courtroom odyssey ended when the Ninth Circuit Court of appeals reaffirmed its earlier decision and ordered the teacher rehired with back pay.

William Rusher, publisher of the conservative *National Review*. As Watergate figures such as John Dean, Charles Colson, and Seattle's John Ehrlichman became household names, the groundswell of public shock mounted, finally forcing a tearful but unrepentant Nixon to resign in 1974.

The impeachment campaign helped change the public image of ACLU from that of an organization which filed legal briefs to one that could wield political clout. Perhaps the most striking demonstration of the ACLU-W's growing clout was a series of campaigns waged over many years. A multifaceted strategy of litigation, legislative lobbying, and public education got results in an area of repeated civil liberties problems: police practices.

Police Brutality

For years the ACLU-W collected information on alleged incidents of police brutality in Seattle. Typical was a statement of a young Black man harassed while waiting at a bus stop in the Central Area:

> "A police car pulled up in front of me, and an officer jumped out and told me to get in. So I turned around real quick. Then the officer pushed me and knocked me down on the ground . . . then the officer's partner got out and ran to help him handcuff me. They started hitting me. (Then) they took me to jail . . ."

In 1955 Mayor Pomeroy formed an Advisory Committee on Police Practices to investigate such complaints. Three ACLU members served on the group, which issued a report noting, "The Police Department is in reality an autonomous branch of city government responsible to no one." Yet no action resulted.

In 1960 the ACLU-W began calling for a "civilian review board" that would serve as an independent body to examine charges of police brutality. Evidence mounted to support allegations by the ACLU-W and other civil rights groups that there was a pattern of brutality, racism, and unlawful acts by police officers. Attorney Phil Burton, an ACLU board member active with the National Association for the Advancement of Colored People, han-

dled the cases of several Blacks beaten by police. When he sued the
Seattle Police Department to obtain files of individual officers, he
was distressed to find the documents made no mention of the
assaults officers had committed. The problem seemed beyond the
reach of litigation.

In 1965 the ACLU-W took the issue directly to the Seattle City
Council. Board president Al Ziontz and executive director Dave
Guren presented a series of affidavits from people who themselves
had been beaten or had witnessed others assaulted by police. The
Council responded by sponsoring highly publicized hearings in
which the civil liberties group presented its evidence of police
abuses. Some of the most devastating testimony was provided by a
former Police Department night clerk who said he had witnessed

Black Panther Party supporters rally at Public Safety Building in Seattle, 1968. *Seattle Times.*

many episodes of brutality, theft, and drunkenness by the police. Al Ziontz told the Council that, "Apparently any so-called back talk from a prisoner triggers violence. The most inflammatory statement a prisoner can make to a Seattle policeman is 'I know my constitutional rights.'" Police Chief Frank Ramon denied the charges, claiming that such complaints were ploys by criminal defense attorneys or retaliation by people who had been arrested.

Despite all the evidence presented, the City Council rebuffed demands by the ACLU-W and others for the creation of a civilian review board and took no action to improve police accountability. But the hearings had shined a public spotlight on police misconduct. Subsequent revelations of widespread payoffs and kickbacks led to the resignation and indictment of some police officials.

Shootings of Blacks by police officers heightened police-community tensions in the Central Area. In 1967, with rumors of an impending race riot filling the air, ACLU-W leaders met with police officials to urge them not to use dragnet arrests and to insure speedy bail. On one particularly tense weekend, the civil liberties group mobilized 50 lawyers to be on call; fortunately, they were not needed. In 1968 the organization opened an office in the Central Area. Among its clients were members of the Black Panther Party. With their defiant demeanor — asserting the right to carry guns, calling for people to "Off the Pigs" — Panthers often clashed with police. In one instance, the ACLU-W won acquittal of a Panther who claimed police had set him up by planting stolen goods at Party headquarters.

In succeeding years, the ACLU-W continued to assist victims of harassment, winning some individual cases but failing to reform Police Department practices. The 1972 ACLU-W Annual Report lamented that police misconduct was generating the largest number of calls to the office. A new dispute arose two years later with a proposal that the Seattle Police Department add hollow point bullets to its arsenal. Led by Executive Director Lauren Selden, the ACLU-W was the first group to denounce the proposal. Representatives of the group conducted extensive research on the issue and met with city officials to express their concern. Nevertheless Mayor Wes Uhlman authorized use of the powerful bullets.

Under pressure from the ACLU-W and Black community groups, however, the City Council agreed to hold hearings on the controversy. Critics charged that the proposal to use hollow points had been based on poor research and that a policy change which would dramatically increase police firepower had been treated as a routine administrative decision. In 1975 the Council took the precedent-setting action of declaring that all issues related to use of deadly force are matters of public policy to be decided by the Council itself, not the police. Council members voted to grant use of low-velocity hollow points, then set velocity limitations on police ammunition.

Thus, public accountability for the police, the principle for which the ACLU-W had long fought, was finally established. The civil liberties group had played a key role in raising and pushing the issue; indeed, the final Council resolution was almost precisely the one framed by the ACLU months earlier. The incident marked a turning point in relations with police, as the ACLU had shown it was a voice to be listened to in setting police policy. Symbolizing this change, Police Chief Robert Hanson appeared on a panel with Al Ziontz at the 1975 annual meeting and answered questions from the ACLU-W audience. Two years later police officials participated in a series of 10 ACLU-sponsored police-community dialogues around the state which used role-playing skits to dramatize law enforcement conflicts.

Police Spying

Authorities had long assumed the right to monitor the activities of radical organizers. In 1956 the Seattle Police Department had been among the first to establish a secretive "Subversive Activities Unit." But revelations about government surveillance of anti-war and militant Black groups in the 1960s showed the risks to political freedoms that police intelligence gathering could pose. And the Watergate scandal of the early 1970s convinced much of the public that officials were going far beyond reasonable bounds. This time, unlike the McCarthy era, the citizenry would not condone wholesale snooping.

In 1969 police officers photographed people marching in a peace demonstration in Longview. The march was nonviolent, and no one was charged with any crime arising from it. Yet police refused to destroy the photos or to hand them over to the marchers. ACLU-W cooperating attorney Jim Gorham sued in Federal District Court on behalf of 10 people who had been photographed, charging the police action was taken to harass and intimidate the plaintiffs from exercising their free speech rights. In 1972 Longview police agreed to a consent order to destroy the negatives and photos of the peaceful marchers.

In 1975 the American Friends Service Committee (AFSC) initiated a national project on police spying in five cities, including Seattle. The AFSC, the National Lawyers Guild, and the ACLU-W formed a Coalition on Government Spying housed in the ACLU's Smith Tower office. The timing was ideal. During confirmation hearings for new police chief Robert Hanson, the *Seattle Post-Intelligencer* obtained and published a list of over a hundred people and groups which the police department had just removed from their intelligence files. Among those named was an assortment of lawyers, liberals, and ministers, including such prominent figures and groups as City Council member Michael Hildt, the Church Council of Greater Seattle, and the Washington Democratic Council. Hanson later admitted to having destroyed 738 "improper" files.

With Betty St. Clair as coordinator, the Coalition worked to get police to reveal the other files that the intelligence unit still maintained. The Coalition organized activists to request their files under the state's Public Disclosure Act. When the police refused to release the files, the Coalition filed a lawsuit handled by attorneys Jim Douglas, Larry Baker, and Mike Withey on behalf of 42 plaintiffs. Under an order from King County Superior Court Judge Frank Howard, police released the files though usually with significant deletions of material.

The files showed no connections between surveillance targets and any criminal actions but did reveal the sloppiness, inaccuracy and paranoia of the cloak-and-dagger operation. A report on the American Friends Service Committee — a group devoted to pacifism — falsely indicated that an unidentified person was "trying to get some bombs made by an unknown student at the UW and has the promise of AFSC to pay for the costs involved." Another flight of fancy had Chicano activist Roberto Maestas punching pro basketball star Bill Walton in the mouth during an argument; the two men, who were friends, ridiculed the claim. The largest file, 78 pages on the National Lawyers Guild, chronicled such lawful activities as a Guild movie showing, a leafletting at a Bar swearing-in-ceremony, an article written for the *Seattle Times*, and a benefit at a tavern. Repeated use of such words as "suspected" and "reliable information indicates" allowed innuendo to stand for facts.

Several years earlier Mayor Wes Uhlman had responded to the initial furor over police spying by establishing a "blue ribbon panel." The Coalition sharply criticized the panel for its weak recommendation that the police department simply establish some new regulations. Instead, the Coalition convinced the City Council to hold public hearings on the police intelligence unit and assembled a number of citizens to tell their stories of harassment. With Charles Royer's election as mayor, that office became more receptive. After all, as a KING-TV reporter Royer had himself briefly been the subject of an intelligence file. Using the lawsuit's continuing disclosures of irrelevant and erroneous files, the Coalition mobilized broad support for reforming police intelligence operations.

During the same period the Coalition also investigated the Law Enforcement Intelligence Unit (LEIU), an information-sharing system among police intelligence units — the old boys' network in action. The Coalition requested from the police department all its correspondence with the information network. The police released a letter informing the LEIU coordinator in California that because of the Coalition's lawsuit and the mayor's soon-to-be-proposed ordinance, Seattle was sending down all its LEIU files "for safe-keeping." "In effect, the police were shipping files out of state because they didn't trust the courts and their own mayor," explains Kathleen Taylor, who succeeded St. Clair as Coalition coordinator. The revelation made clear the need for more civilian control over the police department.

In 1979, after more than a year of tough negotiating sessions led by Council member Randy Revelle, the Seattle City Council unanimously adopted the Police Investigations Ordinance — the first of its kind in the nation — prohibiting police from collecting political information unless it applied directly to the suspect of a crime. The ordinance provided for a civilian auditor to review police records for compliance. The legislation received national acclaim. The Coalition's Kathleen Taylor, City Council member Randy Revelle, and assistant City Attorney Paul Bernstein were sent to Washington, D.C. to testify about the law before the U.S. House Judiciary Subcommittee on Civil and Constitutional Rights.

The work of the Coalition was an outgrowth of government overreaction to the activism of the 1960s and early 1970s. In the less heated political climate of the 1980s, the ordinance has not been sternly tested. After its passage the Coalition continued to seek information about King County's participation in LEIU. In response to a lawsuit, the County in 1980 released 259 pages of LEIU documents — much of the material never before available to the public anywhere else in the nation.

The Rights Revolution

As part of the era's political ferment, less powerful groups in society took forceful action to improve their status. People under the control of social institutions challenged the power of authorities over them. Minorities expressed pride in their heritage and a new-found sense of solidarity. The activism of Native Americans, Chicano farm workers, women, gays, students and others had significant legal dimensions, as they demanded constitutional rights which long had been denied. This "rights revolution" greatly broadened the scope of issues which concerned civil libertarians. Old positions were re-thought, and traditional doctrines were adapted to new situations.

The ACLU-W took an activist approach to addressing the needs of groups seeking empowerment. It pioneered legal support for Indian treaty fishing rights. It initiated special projects on student rights, legal assistance for farm workers, and conditions in county jails. To extend its reach to poor and minority citizens, the civil liberties group for a short time opened an office in Seattle's Central Area. New committees were formed to advance women's rights, gay rights, and prisoner rights. As Len Schroeter, board president in the mid-1960s, puts it, "these were frontier questions and they blossomed. Every flower had its day."

Indian Fishing Rights

Treaties signed by the U.S. government in the 1850s guaranteed Washington's Indians "the right of taking fish at all usual and accustomed places . . . in common with all citizens of the Territory." In the 1960s Native American activists engaged in a series of bitter, sometimes violent disputes with state officials over fishing rights. The ACLU-W took the side of the Native Americans as a matter of principle early in the conflict, lending legal and moral support to a cause that initially seemed quixotic to much of the public.

To Indians, the treaties were their equivalent to the Constitution and Bill of Rights. For civil libertarians, treaty rights presented a dilemma since they weren't mentioned in the U.S. Constitution. Indian rights advocates related their cause to international law concepts of self-determination. Some ACLU'ers, though, worried about potential conflicts between civil liberties and Indian tribal law. In 1965 the ACLU-W board debated a policy statement on Native American rights after a committee had been unable to reach agreement. One position, articulated by John Goldmark, regarded Indian treaty rights as essentially property rights and hence not a civil liberties issue. An opposing view, advocated by Bill Hanson and Al Ziontz, held that treaty rights should be defended as integral to the survival of Indians as an ethnic minority. The adopted policy recognized Indian needs to maintain a group identity and unique subculture and said the ACLU-W would defend Native American rights on a case-by-case basis, so long as they didn't conflict with basic constitutional principles.

In 1964 Washington Indian activists Hank Adams and Bruce Wilkie asked actor Marlon Brando for help in dramatizing their cause. He in turn contacted the national headquarters to find out what the ACLU was doing on fishing rights and found that the New York office didn't even know about the problem. The Washington affiliate, however, soon became active in defending Indians arrested in "fish-ins," symbolic protests in which activists asserted their treaty rights by trying to use their nets. In one major confrontation at Frank's Landing on the Nisqually River in 1965, a melee ensued when state Fisheries and Game Department officials rammed an Indian boat. The ACLU-W's Al Ziontz, who served on the ACLU's national Indian Rights Committee, defended the arrested activists, arguing that they had been exercising First Amendment and treaty rights and that state officials had initiated the violence. In *State v. McCloud, et al.*, tried in Thurston County District Court, all the defendants were acquitted. Brando was arrested in another fish-in, though charges were dismissed because the prosecutor didn't want to get involved in what he regarded as a

Marlon Brando being arrested at "fish-in" on Puyallup River, 1964.   *Seattle Times.*

publicity stunt.

State officials asserted that they were limiting Indian fishing under regulations designed to promote conservation. The effect was to reserve much of the catch for sports fishermen and to destroy the traditional livelihood of Indians. Washington state courts did not issue decisions upholding Indian rights under treaties with the federal government. In *State v. Moses*, for example, ACLU-W attorneys Bill Hanson and Ed Wood filed a brief appealing the conviction of four Muckleshoot Indians who had gillnetted steelhead in the Green River in 1966. The State Supreme Court turned aside the ACLU argument that the state had no right to regulate the Indians' traditional fishing practices, guaranteed by treaties. Ultimately the U.S. Department of Justice stepped in to resolve the issue, filing a suit in 1970 on behalf of all Indian tribes in Western Washington to uphold the supremacy of Indian fishing rights over Washington State laws. Al Ziontz (acting on his own) represented three tribes in the suit. In the landmark *U.S. v. Washington* decision, U.S. Judge George Boldt in 1974 ruled that Native Americans could take up to 50 percent of the catch at their traditional fishing sites.

Migrant Workers Rights

Farm workers have long suffered from low wages and often abysmal living and working conditions. As migrants performing semi-skilled labor, they have been among the most difficult of workers to organize into unions. In the 1960s the United Farm Workers Union, headed by Cesar Chavez, began a series of bitterly fought battles with growers in California. With the support of nationwide boycott campaigns of lettuce and grapes, the union eventually won contracts raising wages and providing for collective bargaining rights.

In Washington, farm worker organizing centered on the Yakima Valley, with its heavily Chicano labor base. In 1968 United Farm Workers organizers requested assistance from the ACLU-W in establishing a legal aid program. Initially, the civil liberties group had no funds for such a project. But executive director Mike Rosen got it off the ground by assembling several hundred law books donated by the University of Washington Law School, borrowed furniture and typewriters, law students supported by work-study programs, a $2,000 donation by a Seattlite, and a grant from a New York church group. Directed by Charles Ehlert, it provided legal representation in such basic matters as traffic cases and wage claims and distributed bilingual leaflets on legal rights. Ultimately the project led to the establishment of a permanent legal aid program now called Yakima Valley Legal Services.

Many Mexican-American farm workers had never been allowed to vote because they could not speak English. ACLU-W attorneys Charles Ehlert and Ed Wood challenged this literacy requirement, and in *Jiminez v. Naff* the Federal District Court upheld its constitutionality. But soon after, Congress passed the Voting Rights Act of 1970, which forbade literacy tests. The ACLU-W appealed to the U.S. Supreme Court, which ordered the lower court to rehear the case based on the new law. This time, in 1972, the court overturned the language requirement, opening the way for thousands of Chicanos to vote.

Farm owners in Washington, as elsewhere, had traditionally been hostile to union organizers, who they thought promoted worker unrest and raised employee expectations unrealistically. In 1971 United Farm Workers organizer Guadelupe Gamboa and attorney Mike Fox were arrested for trespassing when they tried to distribute union information and give legal advice to workers at a large farm near Walla Walla. ACLU-W attorney Charles Ehlert contended that labor organizers had a right to speak with workers and lawyers had a right to consult with potential clients, even at a privately owned work camp. The state's attorney argued that the property rights of camp owners took precedence over First Amendment rights. A lower court found Gamboa and Fox guilty, but in 1973 the State Supreme Court, in *State v. Fox*, overturned the conviction, thus recognizing the right of migrant workers to meet with people of their own choosing.

Women's Rights

Women, too, were making big strides. Increased participation of women in the work force, as well as dissatisfaction with women's status in the male-dominated social justice movements, gave rise to the women's rights movement in the late 1960s. Feminists served notice they would no longer tolerate second-class treatment. The Declaration of Independence had noted that all *men* were created equal; feminists worked to ensure that the Constitution's guarantees of equal treatment under law were applied to women. The drive for women's equality made a profound impact on numerous aspects of American life, especially the legal system. By the mid-1970s no civil liberties issue was being pressed more vigorously — or winning more victories.

In 1972 Washington's voters adopted an Equal Rights Amendment the state Constitution. The ACLU-W pursued women's rights on several other fronts. After pressure from the civil liberties group, the state's Higher Education Personnel Board changed its regulations to allow women to use sick leave for pregnancy. An ACLU-W *amicus* brief buttressed the decision in *Hanson v. Hutt*, in which the State Supreme Court in 1973 upheld a lower court ruling that denying unemployment compensation to a pregnant woman is unconstitutional. When Aetna Insurance threatened to cancel an unmarried woman's policy because she was living with a man, the ACLU-W sued and the insurance company reversed its decision. In another case involving an ACLU-W *amicus* brief, the State Supreme Court in 1975 ruled in *State v. Koome* that a minor does not need parental consent to obtain an abortion. And in that same year the ACLU-W joined women's groups in successfully lobbying for the passage of a new rape law which sharply limited examination of the victim's sexual history.

A case with a twist to the usual sex discrimination claim involved the rights of a husband following a wife who had moved to take a job. In 1972 Robert Ayers, after finding only temporary work in Richland, relocated to Olympia to be with his spouse, who had found employment there with the state government. The Department of Employment Security determined that he had quit his job in Richland without good reason and imposed a 10-week penalty period before he could collect unemployment compensation. ACLU-W cooperating attorneys William Cullen, Carol Fuller, and Chris Young argued that the penalty constituted sex discrimination since a wife was commonly allowed to terminate *her* job without a penalty period to move with her spouse. In 1975 the State Supreme Court agreed, reversing a Thurston County Superior Court decision.

One of the most dramatic cases ever handled by the ACLU-W was that of Captain Susan Struck, a nurse at McChord Air Force Base in Tacoma. In 1970 the Air Force tried to dismiss her summarily from the service for seeking to have her baby after becoming pregnant; opposed to abortion on religious grounds, Struck wanted to take her accrued leave to have the child, then give it up for adoption and continue her military career. ACLU-W staffers Jan Peterson and Bob Czeisler (who became legal counsel in 1971) sought a stay of discharge until the issue could be heard in court. The order was essential, for once the captain was discharged, the only recourse would be to begin the case all over again via a military administrative hearing, a much less favorable venue. Czeisler recalls that the matter proceeded like an old-time serial, with a convoluted plot and narrow escapes:

"At one point Captain Struck called me on a Friday afternoon to say that she was due to be booted from the Air Force at midnight. I called the U.S. Attorney, who said he was leaving his office at 5:00 and couldn't help. I tried to contact the Ninth Circuit judges but all were out of their chambers. Eventually I reached Chief Judge Duniway at home, and he confirmed my interpretation that the Air Force couldn't discharge Struck for 14 more days.

"Next I got ahold of the commanding officer at Minot, North Dakota — where she had been transferred — at 8:00 via field telephone and told him he'd be in contempt of court if he went through with the discharge. The man said he'd have to contact the Pentagon, which then called me to report that the matter was under advisement. Finally at 10 p.m. — two hours before the deadline — the commanding officer at Minot informed me that he was rescinding the discharge order."

The motion to stay the discharge was appealed all the way to the U.S. Supreme Court, where it was upheld by Justice William O. Douglas. By this time Struck had given birth and was ready to return to work; but the Air Force still claimed she had violated regulations which made pregnancy a basis for automatic discharge. She lost at district court, which regarded the issue as simply a contract which she had violated. After a series of appeals and stays, the U.S. Supreme Court granted *certiorari* (review). The Air Force finally gave up, changing its rules and allowing the first person ever to have given birth in the U.S. armed forces to remain in the military.

The passage in 1972 of the Title IX amendment to the federal Civil Rights Act prohibited educational institutions that receive federal funds from discriminating in programs on the basis of sex. It encouraged challenges to unequal treatment of females in schools, as in the celebrated case of Carol and Delores Darrin of Wishkah Valley High School. Located in a small dairy community in Grays Harbor County, the 100-student school sometimes had a shortage of boys for the football team. So the coach, who had suffered through 18 straight losses, was pleased when the Darrin sisters turned out and proved to be varsity-caliber players.

Two days before the 1973 season's first game, the Washington

Interscholastic Athletic Association (WIAA) forbade the Darrins from participating because of a rule against males and females playing contact sports together. The WIAA claimed that sexually integrated sports teams would mean the death of women's sports. It further contended that contact sports could cause "irreparable injury to the breasts." ACLU-W cooperating attorney John Wolfe and staff counsel Mary Howell disputed the claims and cited both Title IX and the state ERA to charge the WIAA with sex discrimination. In 1975 the State Supreme Court in *Darrin v. Gould* ruled that varsity athletic programs in public schools must be open to women students. But by then Carol was in college, and Delores, having sat out two seasons, was no longer interested in playing football.

In framing policies to end sexual inequality, the ACLU-W sometimes had to wrestle with the difficult balance between dis-

Wishkah Valley High School girls seeking to play varsity football, 1973. *Seattle Post-Intelligencer.*

crimination and freedom of speech. For example, in working with officials to draw up compliance regulations for the state statute barring sex discrimination, civil libertarians had to lobby against a ban on stereotyped portrayals of women in texts; they pointed out that the specific regulation would have amounted to textbook censorship. In the 1980s the Board struggled for nearly a year to develop a policy on sexual harassment. Was it an infringement of free speech rights if verbal harassment was prohibited? Would defense of free speech put the group in the position of supporting an harasser? After long months of impassioned debate the Board of Directors determined that verbal sexual harassment which is accompanied by implications of adverse consequences or which constitutes a pattern that interferes with work performance cannot be covered by free speech protections.

Equally controversial was the question of how the civil liberties group should remedy inequality within its own operations. In 1971 women staffers picketed outside the Smith Tower, carrying signs with such slogans as "Civil Liberties Begin at Home." They complained of sexist attitudes in the ACLU-W office, particularly the fact that women held clerical jobs with lower salaries and performed most of the "shit work" necessary to keep the office functioning. Women proposed that the office operate more like a cooperative in which everyone shared the work and was paid equally. Mary Gallwey, chair of the Personnel Committee, flew in from Pullman and interviewed each staffer separately to get all the perspectives on the grievances. As a result, pay for clerical and secretarial work was raised, some of the most tedious tasks were eliminated, and the committee developed a detailed personnel and grievance policy, including preference for promotions from within.

During its early years the ACLU, both nationally and locally, had been a largely male organization. In Washington there had been leaders such as Mary Farquharson in the 1930s and Hilde Applebaum in the 1950s, but they were the exception. Alice Paine served as ACLU-W delegate to the national Biennial Conference during the 1960s, but through the decade's end no woman had been board president or national board representative. In 1972, only 11 of 47 ACLU-W board members and 6 of 15 chapter chairs were women. As the newsletter noted wryly that year, women's gains in organizational responsibility were "not immense."

In the early 1970s an active Women's Rights Committee chaired by Lynne Iglitzin pushed for organizational change. It sought cases for referral to the Legal Committee and advocated that the organization take them on. A Women's Caucus met for breakfast just before board meetings to discuss strategies for raising both women's issues and status. Women's rights advocates had to grapple with the tension between their commitment to equality and a deeply held conviction that board elections should be free. In 1972 the Women's Rights Committee had suggested that to remedy the gender imbalance there be dual slates of men and women board candidates, with some selected from each so as to make the board's at-large membership 50 percent women. This raised objections to "rigging" elections. Some members also argued that since women made up only a third of the organization's membership, they were already represented fairly on the board. However, the prevailing position recognized that historical factors had produced the pre-dominantly male membership and that the ACLU-W should begin affirmative action where it would be most visible — at the board level. So the board instructed the Nominating Committee to present a board slate that was 60 percent women.

The next spring's elections brought a dramatic change to the board's gender composition. Women were elected to 9 of 12 board vacancies, and Ann Widditsch became the first woman board president. By 1974 women filled a majority of the board's at-large slots. The board also mandated that the next staff counsel be a woman, and Mary Howell was hired. Some longtime board members did not welcome accompanying changes. They felt that the new women, however competent they might be in other spheres, did not have the sophistication about civil liberties which had previously informed board debates. Some women regarded the "quality of debate" issue as a code phrase for a longing for return to the old, heavily male board.

Such a return was not to come. The ACLU-W became a na-tional leader in electing women to leadership positions. Mary Gallwey served an unprecedented four terms (1974-1978) as board president, and she, Ann Widditsch, Kay Frank, and Judy Bendich all served as president and on the national board. Kathleen Taylor was hired as the first full-time woman executive director in 1980. And women would play crucial roles in helping the organization weather a severe financial crisis.

Gay Rights

In 1957 the national Board had determined that it was not the ACLU's role to evaluate the social validity of laws to suppress homosexuals. But the rise of the "gay pride" movement debunked widely held stereotypes about homosexuality and helped civil libertarians realize that discrimination against people for their sexual orientation was indeed a civil liberties concern. The ACLU-W brought the issue out of the closet in 1971 with the formation of a Gay Rights Committee chaired by former staff counsel Chris Young. The civil liberties group backed the Legislature's 1975 repeal of state laws criminalizing private, noncommercial sexual conduct between consenting adults and Seattle's inclusion of sexual orientation in ordinances banning discrimination in employment (1973) and housing (1975). When an ad hoc group calling itself Save Our Moral Ethics filed an initiative to overturn the latter two measures in 1978, voters in Seattle made it the first major American city to defeat an anti-gay rights campaign.

Litigation on discrimination against gays proved arduous. In 1972 John Singer of Seattle lost his job with the Federal Equal Employment Opportunity Commission (a true misnomer in this instance) after publicly advocating gay rights. The Civil Service Commission, Federal District Court, and the Court of Appeals all rebuffed efforts to regain his job. While ACLU-W cooperating attorney Larry Baker and national staff counsel Dave Barnett appealed the case to the U.S. Supreme Court, Federal officials noted that Singer would not have lost his job under new regulations adopted since 1972 at the urging of the ACLU and others. So the Federal Civil Service Commission in 1978 finally ordered Singer reinstated. He had moved out of state by this time, but gladly accepted full back pay.

A celebrated victory involved Madeleine Isaacson and Sandra Schuster and the rights of gay parents in Washington. The lesbian couple had each been awarded custody of her children in 1973 divorces, but with the proviso that the pair maintain separate residences "in the best interests" of the children. When the fathers, now remarried, sought to gain custody in 1974, the ACLU-W filed a counterpetition to end the residence ban. The fathers' attorneys harped on alleged liabilities of gay parents. The mothers' four-person legal team — Alix Foster, Arnie Pedowitz, Julie Herak, and

Rallying for Gay Rights in Seattle, 1977. *Phil Webber.*

Mary Howell — presented psychologists who testified to the children's good emotional health. King County Superior Court Judge Norman Ackley granted the women's petition, ruling that the issue was the fitness of the parents, not their sexuality. In 1978 the State Supreme Court upheld the decision.

Despite legal gains, prejudice against gays persisted in many areas. In 1977 the president of Everett Community College rejected a Gay Students Alliance petition for recognition as an official student organization. He claimed the request was coercive, noting that, "We non-homosexuals are to be forced to live in the conspicuous presence of a deviant behavior which for hundreds of years has been an occasion for fear and an inspiration for violence." ACLU-W cooperating attorneys Bob Gibbs and Bob Beckerman filed suit in Federal court, charging the president's action violated freedom of expression and association as well as equal protection guarantees. Although Judge Donald Voorhees denied a preliminary injunction, he reiterated a now famous phrase that "Students do not shed their First Amendment rights at the schoolhouse gate." Seeing the writing on the wall the college's Board of Trustees voted 3-2 to approve the gay group's charter.

Sadly, a court challenge failed to win a similar victory for a

Tacoma teacher. In 1977 the State Supreme Court upheld the 1972 firing of Jim Gaylord for being gay. Though Gaylord had compiled an excellent record during 12 years in the classroom, the Court found that the mere fact of acknowledging his homosexuality rendered Gaylord "immoral" and therefore unfit to teach. An equally unfortunate ruling involved a U.S. soldier. In 1979, the U.S. Army revoked the security clearance of Sergeant Perry Watkins for admitting his homosexuality. After the ACLU-W's Jim Lobsenz began representing him in an appeal, the Army moved to have Watkins discharged. In 1982 Judge Barbara Rothstein ruled that the sergeant couldn't be ousted for his sexual orientation. But two years later the Ninth Circuit Court of Appeals reversed her decision, saying that the Federal Court judge lacked authority to overrule the military. (As of summer, 1987, an appeal of the case was still pending on grounds that Watkins had been denied equal protection of the law.)

Student Rights

In 1966 eighth-grader Tom Poll was suspended from classes in North Shore School District for having hair which touched his eyebrows. Officials said it violated school standards for good grooming. The suspension came the day before the 13-year-old's scheduled induction into the Honor Society. The ACLU-W obtained a temporary restraining order, and Poll, accompanied by his parents and flanked by two attorneys with a court order, took part in the induction ceremony. While the ACLU's challenge to the hair length regulation lost in King County Superior Court, so many students grew their hair long over the summer that officials were unable to enforce the regulation next fall.

Challenges to school policies grew common in the late 1960s. Sometimes they entailed mass protest, as when 150 students walked out of class at Seattle's Shorecrest High after the shooting of students at Kent State University. More often they stemmed simply from an individual's personal appearance, as in Tom Poll's case. Used to running academic affairs without being questioned, administrators often overreacted with arbitrary suspensions. Civil libertarians insisted that the Constitution applied within the

ACLU-W member Orabelle Poll with son Tom, 13, wearing the haircut that got him suspended from school, 1966. *Seattle Post-Intelligencer.*

schoolhouse — that students, insofar as practical, be granted rights
to freedom of expression and hearings to review disciplinary
actions.

The ACLU-W became involved in a wide variety of school
issues — disputes over haircuts, dress codes, anti-war activism
and underground newspapers. So numerous were complaints of
abuses that in 1970 the organization sponsored a year-long Student
Rights Project directed by Jan Peterson. Much of the work didn't
involve litigation. Peterson put on educational programs around
the state to inform students and parents of their rights. He and
other ACLU'ers mediated disputes between principals and students, headed off problems with phone calls to administrators, and

represented students in disciplinary hearings.

Because students questioned traditional community standards of behavior, school conflicts were often highly emotional. In 1969, for example, the ACLU's Dave Taylor represented Charles Sturdevent, a Lacey high schooler suspended for long hair. At a hearing the North Thurston School Board voted to readmit Sturdevent and to abolish his school's vague haircut rule. Irate parents staged a write-in campaign that ousted two school boardmembers who had voted for the student. In the face of such intense pressure some parents and students declined to pursue their cases. In 1969 the ACLU-W obtained a temporary restraining order to stop the suspension of a 14-year-old student with long hair in the small town of White Pass. After receiving numerous threats and newspaper smears, his parents decided to drop the case.

Underlying students rights controversies was the question of what sorts of conduct could legitimately be regarded as disrupting school. In the landmark *Tinker v. Des Moines* decision, the U.S Supreme Court ruled in 1969 that Iowa students who had worn black armbands to protest the Vietnam War were engaging in acts of free speech that did not disrupt the functioning of school. Longtime ACLU-W board member Mary Gallwey recalls that local school administrators were often slow to recognize the principle:

> "Shortly after *Tinker* was handed down, I heard that Colfax High School in southeastern Washington was barring from school students wearing black armbands to protest the war. I called the principal and said that perhaps he was unaware that this very issue had recently been decided by the Supreme Court. I even read him a section of the decision. He told me 'I don't care what the Supreme Court says — it doesn't apply in my school.' He informed me that all his teachers had fought in World War II and didn't approve of anti-war protests.
>
> "We discussed the incident with the student ACLU chapter at Washington State University. Some students went to leaflet at the high school, handing out copies of the Bill of Rights and portions of the *Tinker* decision on the sidewalk in front of school. A teacher who objected to the action asked them, 'Don't you know you can be sued for plagiarism?' Without batting an eyelash, a student re-

sponded, 'Who has the copyright on the Bill of Rights?'

In the end the principal did acknowledge to the students that he had been wrong and apologized. They were admitted to school with their armbands."

Student rights issues had to be fought district-by-district or even school-by-school because each district was independent. In 1970 Tom Hodges came to the ACLU when he was suspended from Seattle's Ingraham High School for handing out political leaflets without prior approval by the principal. A King County Superior Court judge upheld the school's limitation on distributing political literature from groups outside the school, but an appeal became moot when the district changed its regulations to allow free speech rights to leafletters. ACLU-W staff counsel Chris Young obtained a hearing before the Seattle School Board for Cleveland High School students suspended for forming a Black Student Union. A subsequent proposal by Young paved the way for the Board to take a key action by adopting district-wide guidelines setting forth student rights, including procedures for discipline and appeal that incorporated due process principles.

Gains also were made in the right to symbolic freedom of expression. In 1970 the ACLU-W represented Rocky Nelson, a student suspended from Mossyrock High in Lewis County because administrators claimed his long hair was hazardous in an Agricultural Mechanics class. A Superior Court judge ruled the suspension illegal and ordered Nelson readmitted, providing he wore a safety device in the class. In 1970 Jan Peterson of the ACLU-W filed suit for Maryanne Stroud, a young women who was suspended from Lakes High School in Tacoma for wearing pants to school; the attorney charged the school's dress code violated the equal protection clause of the Fourteenth Amendment since boys were allowed to wear pants to class. Before the case reached court, the school adopted a new dress code allowing female students to wear slacks and pants. The volume of student rights cases tapered off in the mid-1970s as school protests died down, administrators became more tolerant of changed hair and dress standards, and due process rights replaced summary suspensions.

Rights of the Poor

Jerry Mempa, 17, had been arrested for "joy-riding" in 1959 and was put on probation. A few months later his probation officer alleged that Mempa had been involved in a burglary. At the probation revocation hearing his request for a court-appointed attorney was denied, and he was not allowed to cross-examine witnesses or even make a statement in his defense. Not surprisingly, Mempa received a lengthy prison term. In 1965 he filed a petition for *habeas corpus* to the State Supreme Court charging that his confinement violated the Constitution. After the Court rejected his plea, the ACLU-W's Mike Rosen and Evan Schwab petitioned for and the U.S. Supreme Court granted a writ of *certiorari* (review of constitutionality). In 1967, in *Mempa v. Rhay*, the high court accepted 9-0 the ACLU contention that an indigent has the right to counsel at a probation revocation hearing.

Nominally, all citizens have the same rights under the law. In practice, poverty often has prevented people from receiving equal

---

Freedom from Harassment: The Love Arts Sale Incident

In 1967 the Seattle Committee to End the War in Vietnam staged a three-day "Love Arts Sale" to raise funds. The City License Department quickly closed down the affair, claiming its sponsors needed four different permits. ACLU-W cooperating attorney John Caughlan asked for an immediate hearing. After a two-hour meeting with officials, they agreed with his contention that the city's charitable solicitation ordinance was being unconstitutionally applied to a political fundraising event. The fair reopened.

Three hours later the Fire Department shut down the event. Caughlan quickly arranged a meeting with the Fire Chief. "You can smell a fire a mile away," the attorney told him. "Well, I think I can smell something having to do with harassment." The Chief claimed there had been no intent to harass and the closure had been a mistake. The Love Arts Sale again reopened, this time continuing without incident.

treatment in the judicial system. Civil libertarians have pointed out that defendants who face criminal charges and can't afford an attorney must be provided one by the court if they are to have a fair trial. In the late 1960s and early 1970s, the ACLU-W pursued several cases to establish the rights of indigents to legal counsel.

Leon Hendrix of Seattle had been convicted of a misdemeanor. ACLU-W cooperating attorney John Junker appealed the conviction, saying the defendant had been denied due process because he had lacked an attorney; Junker argued that in a "serious" misdemeanor — one involving a possible jail term — counsel must be provided. A King County Superior Court judge agreed, but in 1969 the Washington State Supreme Court overturned that decision by a 5-4 vote. Three years later the U.S. Supreme Court accepted this principle in the landmark *Argersinger v. Hamlin* case. The decision cited, among other things, a law review article written by Junker, a University of Washington Law School professor. In another case, *Honore v. Washington Board of Prison Terms and Paroles*, Junker argued that a prisoner filing a *habeas corpus* petition should have the right to counsel; the Washington State Supreme Court accepted this principle in 1970.

Another issue that affected poor people in particular was the handling of public drunkenness. Wayne Jacob Hill was convicted in 1966 of public intoxication near Seattle's Pioneer Square. ACLU-W cooperating attorneys Luvern Rieke and Arnold Barer appealed, arguing that chronic alcoholism was an illness and that it was cruel and unusual punishment to incarcerate one for displaying symptoms of an illness. The State Supreme Court rejected the appeal on the grounds that since Hill had a home, he didn't *have* to be drunk in public. Hill died in the Seattle City Jail in 1969, having been arrested 156 times for drunkenness in the previous 20 years. Legislators in Olympia realized that many transients, unlike Hill, had no choice but to do their drinking in public. In the early 1970s the Legislature adopted the Uniform Alcoholism and Intoxication Treatment Act, providing for medical treatment rather than jailing of people for drunkenness.

Rights of the Mentally Ill

Traditionally the state has had the power to commit mentally ill citizens to psychiatric hospitals against their will. In the 1960s the writings of Thomas Szasz and others sparked much discussion about the nature of mental illness and the value of depriving the mentally ill of their liberty, especially without guarantees of fair hearings. The ACLU-W, under the prodding of psychologist and longtime board member Art Kobler, was a major force in reforming Washington's mental commitment policies.

A nightmarish incident in Seattle demonstrated the danger of ignoring due process rights. In 1968 Daniel Anderson was arrested for pulling a burglar alarm while on a "speed trip." After he asked to telephone "the white house on Capitol Hill," referring to his home in Seattle's Capitol Hill neighborhood, police, thinking he wished to call the U.S. President, transferred him to a psychiatric ward. Although the ACLU-W had requested that he not be drugged prior to his hearing, he was under heavy sedation during the proceeding and appeared mentally unstable. A judge committed him to the psychiatric unit of a Veterans Administration hospital, where he received electro-convulsive shock treatment. After six months he escaped by crawling through a window and contacted ACLU-W cooperating attorney Landon Estep. Ruling on a suit by Estep, King County Superior Court Judge James Mifflin in 1969 found that the commitment order had been unconstitutional since Anderson had been provided neither a guardian nor an attorney.

The ACLU brought several suits challenging the lack of due process in the state's commitment procedures. In another key case, cooperating attorney Landon Estep challenged the involuntary commitment of Joyce Quesnell. No evidence had been presented to show that Quesnell was dangerous or had a mental disease. No attorney had been provided, nor had the patient been allowed to cross-examine her accusers, call her own medical witnesses, or even be present at the hearing. King County Superior Court Judge Horton Smith ordered a rehearing with an attorney and cross-examination of witnesses, a ruling later upheld by the Washington State Supreme Court.

Estep helped draft a revision of the state's mental commitment statute, and the ACLU-W's legal director Bob Czeisler lobbied for its passage. In 1973 the Legislature enacted the ACLU-supported

Involuntary Treatment Act. It limited the scope of the state's commitment authority to people with "a likelihood of serious harm to themselves or others" or who were themselves "gravely disabled." The statute also set up procedural safeguards to end indefinite commitment and to shorten the length of hospital detentions.

Prisoner Rights

When Mike Rosen started work as ACLU-W staff counsel in 1965, he found piles of unanswered letters from prisoners — over 250 in all. Many inmates had very specific needs for help with appeals of their conviction or *habeas corpus* petitions. An overall problem, though, was that most jail administrators acted as if the Bill of Rights didn't apply to the incarcerated. The ACLU-W responded by focusing on cases which involved significant infringements of civil liberties and in which it could make an impact. For example, officials at Walla Walla Penitentiary were refusing to allow Black Muslim inmates to meet with religious leaders or receive their faith's literature. In 1971 cooperating attorney Charles Routh obtained a directive from the State Attorney General guaranteeing the Muslims the right to practice their religion behind bars. After the deluge of prison letters had continued for several years, the ACLU-W established in 1972 a Prisoner Rights Committee chaired by Jim Herrick.

The next year the ACLU-W initiated a County Jail Project through which the group's representatives visited 25 jails around the state. These inspectors found jail conditions that were "substandard and unhumane" and observed a pattern of prisoner beatings, banned newspapers, and censored mail. "Power is often exercised arbitrarily and capriciously," they reported. The Project's report was circulated among sheriffs, county commissioners, Superior Court judges, and local press. It spurred the creation of a State Jail Commission and its successor, the Corrections Standards Board, which monitored jail conditions.

The ACLU-W joined with Legal Services in 1974 to sue Snohomish County Jail officials over a whole set of repressive practices. The jail staff had banned all newspapers, censored magazines, read attorney-client mail, refused to mail legal proceedings prepared by inmates, and punished prisoners by beating them and placing them nude in "the hole," an isolation tank. Several jailers had established a reign of terror, choking, hitting, and kicking prisoners. ACLU and Legal Services attorneys took up the challenge. Hoping to avoid a court battle, a new sheriff and the county's superior court judges, who were responsible for overseeing jail conditions, negotiated for seven months to reach an agreed order for dismissal. Under new jail rules "the hole" was closed, corporal punishment was forbidden, mail censorship was greatly curtailed, and newspapers were provided to prisoners. In related changes some jailers were fired, and social workers were hired.

Despite these improvements, conditions remained deplorable for some of the state's prisoners. During a month-long lockdown at Walla Walla Penitentiary in 1979, the ACLU-W received a torrent of phone calls and letters from prisoners complaining of brutality by guards, racism, destruction of personal property, denial of access to counsel, and lack of adequate health care. Built in 1887 to house 850 prisoners, it was now warehousing 1,600 people, with four men often crammed into cells 10 feet long and eight feet wide. The severe overcrowding caused tensions which sparked a riot and

Walla Walla Penitentiary during prisoners' strike, 1970.   *Seattle Post-Intelligencer.*

in turn led to brutal assaults on prisoners. "Can you help us? We are not animals," implored one inmate's letter.

To remedy the situation ACLU-W cooperating attorney Tim Ford, Evergreen Legal Services, and other attorneys filed a complex lawsuit on behalf of Walla Walla inmates against Governor Dixy Lee Ray, several state officials, and a host of corrections officers. The class-action suit held officials responsible for the violence and intolerable treatment during the lockdown, as well as the incendiary conditions which sparked the riot. In *Hoptowit v. Ray* Judge Jack Tanner of the U.S. District Court in Spokane ruled that the "totality of conditions" at the prison violated the Eighth Amendment's protection against cruel and unusual punishment. He ordered the state to implement a set of remedies to alleviate overcrowding and upgrade medical care, guard behavior, and conditions in custody, isolation, and segregation units. The judge also ordered that a Master be appointed to oversee reform of the prison's operations.

The case dragged on through a lengthy appeal process. In 1982 the Ninth Circuit Court of Appeals upheld key parts of Tanner's rulings but rejected others, including the order for a Master. By 1985, when a revised decision by Tanner was upheld, the state had spent millions of dollars to improve many of the conditions, though the overcrowding remained.

Challenge and Maturity

Crisis

The late 1960s had been a time of unprecedented expansion. From 1965 to 1971 the membership and budget of the ACLU-W had more than doubled. Full-time executive directors and staff counsels were hired, the legal docket swelled, and special projects, such as an office in the Central Area, a legal aid program in the Yakima Valley, and a student rights education campaign, were initiated. Unfortunately the group's finances failed to keep pace with its growing program. A deficit that began as a few thousand dollars accumulated to a worrisome $25,000 by 1970 and a staggering $40,000 in 1972 — a full 40 percent of that year's budget. The debt peaked at $64,000 in 1975, threatening the ACLU-W's very survival. For several years money problems caused continuing anxiety and consumed an unhealthy share of the organization's energies.

How had an affiliate which a few years earlier had been an organizational model for the national ACLU gotten itself in such a deep hole? Several factors were at work. For one, the prosperity of the mid-1960s gave way to a recession at the decade's end. The work force of the Boeing Company, the region's largest corporate employer, shrank from 101,000 in 1968 to 37,000 three years later. A billboard reading, "Will the last person leaving Seattle please turn off the lights?" wryly described the situation. Economic stagnation hurt ACLU-W revenue by slowing the increase in new members and forcing many loyal members to cut back their contributions.

At the same time, the group's fundraising methods were inadequate. To be sure, ACLU-W activists brainstormed long and hard over ideas for bringing in money. In 1969 the group staged one of the most successful fundraisers of any affiliate to date, a concert at the Seattle Center Arena featuring the era's hottest folk music group. Peter, Paul, and Mary were invited to Seattle by the ACLU-

W to be given an award for their deep involvement in civil rights work. Hugh Fleetwood, a philosophy professor at Western Washington State College and ACLU-W board president from 1969-1971, recalls that much backstage maneuvering accompanied the concert:

> "Unfortunately, executive director Mike Rosen and I weren't fully candid about the fact that we wanted them to do a concert. When Mike called their agent's secretary to check on details for the concert, there was a long pause before she asked, 'What concert?' A couple days later my home phone rang about midnight. It was Peter, i.e., the folk singer Peter Yarrow. He said that Mary was furious and didn't want to come. I pulled myself together and tried to explain that there had been a series of misunderstandings. The next day I was interrupted in the middle of class by an emergency phone call. It was the agent, and he wanted to know how many tickets had been sold. I told him several thousand. Unwilling to risk alienating that many fans, he agreed that Peter, Paul, and Mary would come.
>
> "When Mary arrived, she was still quite irritated over feeling misused by us. She felt so bitter that she refused to let the trio receive our award. But they did go on with the concert, and we cleared almost $20,000 — an enormous amount for those days."

Yet reliance on one-shot extravaganzas to supplement income from memberships did not provide a stable source of revenue. Organizing rock concerts, film festivals, art sales, and the like took a major amount of time and energy. Many were smashing successes, while some flopped, putting the group even farther in the hole. Several more years of hustling for money, of trying to pull rabbits out of hats would pass until the ACLU-W institutionalized annual fundraising programs.

The biggest cause of the dangerous debt was that the organization did not manage its fiscal affairs in a businesslike manner. There were no long-range planning, no reserves, no balance sheets, no auditing, no system of financial controls. On one occasion board members were horrified to find a pile of unpaid bills crammed into the desk drawer of a recently departed executive director. Another

time Social Security and withholding taxes for staff were not paid,
leaving the group with a substantial debt to that most demanding of
creditors, the Internal Revenue Service. Budgets grew like Topsy,
from $76,000 in 1970 to a record $130,000 two years later. Typically
expenditures were pegged to rosy forecasts of income which didn't
pan out. As a result, the group was simply living beyond its means.
As Rose Marie Van Winkle, a board member in the mid-1970s,
observes, "It was like running the Federal government, except we
couldn't print money."

The prevailing mindset was to set high financial goals, then
strive to reach them. This approach had worked in the early 1960s
but was a dubious *modus operandi* a decade later. Board members
tended to be idealists, deep in their commitment to civil liberties,
but short on fiscal skills. Executive directors had to bear the burden of fundraising and sometimes did not make monetary information readily available to the board. Board members and staff
alike had a hard time saying "no" to new programs. As former
board president Hugh Fleetwood notes, "Those were yeasty days
for civil libertarians. We were always acting under the impulse to
expand. We saw enormous needs. Change was required, and by
God, we were going to do it. It took a long time for financial
responsibility to set in." A major accomplishment came in 1972
when the board faced up to fiscal reality by axing $30,000 from that
year's $130,000 budget.

Yet in February of 1975 the *Seattle Post-Intelligencer* warned of the
imminent collapse of the ACLU-W. Reports of its demise proved
premature as the organization took several steps which turned the
tide. Debts were consolidated, and the staff position of legal counsel
was eliminated after Mary Howell left. Recruitment campaigns
brought in hundreds of new members, and a special $25 assess-
ment of members pulled in thousands of dollars. A group of dedicated members, many of them women, played critical roles, taking
over work previously done by paid staff, lending the organization
money, and negotiating with creditors. Mary Gallwey recalls telling one who threatened to sue, "You can press this in court, but you
won't satisfy your debt and we'll be out of existence." Rose Marie
Van Winkle was appointed financial officer in 1975 with the responsibility for overseeing the day-to-day handling of fiscal affairs.
Alice Phillips and Herdis Benediktson put in untold hours of vol-

unteer work at the office.

The final storm came in 1978. "Help! . . . May Day . . . SOS . . . Emergency" pleaded the front-page headline of the June ACLU-W newsletter. An urgent appeal for money explained that although the group had retired $40,000 of its debt in the previous four years, it had run out of money for current operations. Expenses had increased, membership had temporarily declined. And a highly emotional case grabbed headlines.

In 1977 the ACLU had made one of its most controversial decisions: to defend the right of American Nazis to march through the Chicago suburb of Skokie. To most citizens the march of virulent anti-Semites through a heavily Jewish community was an outrage and a provocation. For the ACLU to assist such people seemed to align the group with despicable elements of society who had contempt for the democratic rights of others. Yet ACLU leaders saw in the Nazi march a basic First Amendment issue. As national ACLU director Aryeh Neier put it, "If the ACLU does not maintain fidelity to the principle that free speech must be defended for all, we do not deserve to exist or to call ourselves a civil liberties organization. Caving in to a hostile reaction — some of it from

---

Resisting the Abuse of Power: The Chambless Case

At a 1970 anti-war demonstration outside Seattle's Federal Courthouse, activists John and Dorothy Chambless attempted to stop what later turned out to be a plainclothes policeman from dragging a protester by the neck. The couple were arrested for interfering with an officer. In Seattle Municipal Court, ACLU-W staff counsel Jan Peterson argued that the defendants hadn't known the plainclothesman was a police officer. However, the officer claimed to have identified himself by flashing his ID card. In a dramatic ploy, Peterson asked the man to grab him by the neck with one hand and then try to pull out his ID card from a back pocket with the other. The cop's fumbling attempt cast serious doubt on his story, and after a five-hour trial — the longest in the history of the Municipal Court to that time — both John and Dorothy Chambless were acquitted.

ACLU members — would only advance the notion that speakers may be silenced if listeners are offended."

Many ACLU members were disturbed by their organization's position. Indeed, the summer after the Skokie affair, ACLU-W president Mary Gallwey found that a goodly number of nonrenewals of membership had been motivated by dissatisfaction with the defense of the Nazis' rights. She and others personally contacted lapsed members to explain the civil liberties principle involved. They pointed out that the Nazis had chosen to march in Skokie after being refused permits to assemble in parks in and around Chicago unless they obtained an unreasonably large amount of liability insurance.

The Washington affiliate had recently challenged a similar provision in Tacoma's parade ordinance. When the Pierce County Women's Coalition had sought to hold a parade celebrating women's suffrage, Tacoma authorities insisted the group obtain $300,000 in liability insurance against damage which might result from spectators aroused over the right of women to vote. ACLU-W cooperating attorneys Lee Raaen and Bob Beckerman argued that the city's actions were illegal and presented evidence that a bed race had been allowed through Tacoma streets without any insurance requirement. A U.S. District Court judge granted an injunction enabling the women's group to hold their parade. When the ACLU-W threatened further litigation, the Tacoma City Council adopted a new ordinance dropping the insurance requirement. Quite a few people rejoined the ACLU-W after they realized the underlying principle in Tacoma and Skokie was the same.

The ACLU-W weathered the 1978 crisis, again through the efforts of deeply committed members. They called individuals who had supported the ACLU and solicited money to keep the phones going. Several board members made no-interest loans to cover debts. For seven months after the departure of David Harrison in 1978, the group functioned without an executive director. A committee of Kay Frank, Mary Gallwey, and Rose Marie Van Winkle met frequently at the Smith Tower office with staff members Marsha Weese and Judy Andrews to deal with routine organizational matters. The group relied on government employment programs such as CETA for staff to perform essential office work. Through the combination of emergency measures and better financial management the ACLU-W not only managed to survive, but by the end of 1980 was finally out of debt.

Keeping the Faith

The money crunch strained operations in many ways. Staff and board time that should have gone into programs was spent agonizing about how to cope with the deficit. An air of uncertainty dampened staff morale, and turnover of personnel was rapid — 100 percent between 1972 and 1973. Corners had to be cut in running the office. David Harrison, who became ACLU-W executive director in 1976 after holding the same position in Vermont, recalls asking for a pencil soon after his arrival. "Sorry, I'll bring some from home," replied volunteer Alice Phillips.

Yet despite the constraints the ACLU-W moved forward with a substantial program. Michelle Pailthorp coordinated lobbying efforts that brought pressure to bear on numerous legislative proposals in Olympia. In 1977 the ACLU-W cosponsored a daylong conference at the University of Washington on how citizens could make use of the Freedom of Information Act. The next year the Women's Rights Committee cosponsored the state's first Continuing Legal Education seminar devoted solely to women's rights. Also in 1978 the ACLU-W began a year-long Project on Age Discrimination. Headed by Bob Beckerman and Marnie Walters, it challenged mandatory retirement, raised public awareness of the need for fair treatment of the aged, and published a booklet ("Age Equality") on age discrimination. The organization also maintained an active legal docket which mixed traditional civil liberties issues with newer ones raised by the Rights Revolution.

In 1976 the administration of Eastern Washington State College barred a fraternity from showing the film *Deep Throat* on campus because it was deemed "not in furtherance of the educational purposes of the institution." Spokane County Superior Court accepted cooperating attorney Fred Schuchart's contention that the ban was an unconstitutional prior restraint on freedom of expression. In 1977 the ACLU-W's Tim Ford sued to stop the practice by Skamania County School District of having students run a gauntlet to get spanked by other students. School officials were forced to drop the disciplinary measure which violated state laws on corporal punishment. The ACLU-W also challenged the 1976 felony conviction of Everett's Jim Smith for growing marijuana plants in his garage for home use. The argument that a felony sentence for such a minor transgression was cruel and unusual punishment swayed several judges, but the State Supreme Court in 1980, in *Smith v. State*, upheld the conviction in a 5-4 ruling.

Opposition to the death penalty as cruel and unusual punishment had long been a tenet of civil libertarians. In 1965 the ACLU-W had voted to oppose capital punishment both in principle, for allowing for no remedy should new evidence turn up, and in practice, for being much more likely to be applied to minorities and the poor. Staff counsel Mike Rosen and cooperating attorney John Junker challenged the death sentence for James Hawkins, who had written the ACLU-W from death row two weeks before his scheduled execution. After a series of stays, the State Supreme Court in 1970 overturned the death penalty for Hawkins because people opposed to capital punishment had been excluded from his trial jury.

During the 1970s the civil liberties group remained active on the issue. In the 1975 Legislature the ACLU-W played a major role in persuading lawmakers to kill a bill to reinstitute the death penalty in Washington. The organization assembled Citizens Against Hanging, an ad hoc coalition of civil rights and religious groups directed by Troy Locati and Tim Ford which opposed a statewide death penalty ballot measure. Initiative 316 passed easily in 1976 but was invalidated a year later in a suit brought by Tim Ford (acting on his own) on grounds that it made the death penalty mandatory in certain cases. The Legislature passed another capital punishment bill in 1977, but it, too, was thrown out by the courts in 1981 in another Tim Ford suit on grounds that it only applied to defendants who pleaded not guilty. The death penalty law currently in force in Washington was adopted by the Legislature in 1981 and has withstood court challenges.

The previously discussed Coalition on Government Spying was another major initiative the ACLU-W was able to undertake despite its financial woes. And in this same difficult period in the mid-1970s the ACLU, with other civil rights groups, served as a catalyst to force Seattle's education system to face up to a problem it had ducked for years.

School Desegregation

Ending racially segregated schools was a major goal of the civil rights movement. In 1954 the U.S. Supreme Court had ruled in the landmark *Brown v. Board of Education* case that "separate but equal" schools were no longer acceptable. The decision removed official sanction from *de jure* segregation, that is, discrimination backed by law. Tackling *de facto* segregation, discrimination arising from a community's structure (e.g., Black inner cities and White neighborhoods and suburbs), presented more difficulties.

Under pressure from civil rights groups the Seattle School Board adopted a voluntary racial transfer program. Dissatisfied, Black community groups in 1966 organized a school boycott in support of comprehensive desegregation. School officials indicated they would take action, prompting the National Association for the Advancement of Colored People (NAACP) to withdraw a suit it had filed to compel desegregation. In 1970 the School Board adopted a mandatory busing program but only for middle schools. As the decade proceeded, the School Board twice postponed deadlines for eliminating segregation throughout the entire school system.

The issue was a divisive one for civil libertarians. In 1966 the ACLU-W board adopted by an 8-7 vote a policy declaring that *de facto* segregation violated the equal protection clause of the Fourteenth Amendment. Some opponents of this position argued that *de facto* segregation was a social problem, not a civil liberties issue, since it did not result from government action. Others objected to pegging the problem to the Fourteenth Amendment, saying that a solution should be pursued through the political process rather than by trying "to stretch" the Bill of Rights.

A decade later, as the civil liberties group discussed a report by its Committee on Seattle School Desegregation chaired by Jim Tyler, the terms of the debate had shifted. Now the dispute was over the possible conflict between ending segregation via busing and achieving quality education. Some ACLU-W board members based their stance on traditional civil rights doctrine, as expressed in the *Brown* decision, that racially segregated schools were inherently unequal. Allowing such schools to exist, they added, simply perpetuated racism. Others contended that mandatory transfers unduly disrupted the educational process, and that providing a sound education for all children was more important than moving

Riding the bus to a desegregated school in Seattle, 1978.   *Seattle Times.*

students around. Al Ziontz pointed out the need to consider feed-
back from some members of the Black community who felt that
forced transfers to ensure racial balance diluted the quality of
Central Area schools. "Our first task is to integrate the school
system and worry about what constitutes quality education later,"
retorted board member Lauren Selden. "We must have integration
even if it means coercing social change on those who resist it."

In 1976, despite divisions over timing, the ACLU-W board
adopted a resolution urging the Seattle School Board to take
prompt action to achieve racial balance in all the district's schools.
"The continued existence of racially identifiable schools is intolerable," proclaimed its statement. Under the leadership of executive
director David Harrison, the ACLU-W plunged into the campaign
to end school segregation. The ACLU joined with the NAACP and
the Church Council of Greater Seattle in threatening to sue the
Seattle School Board for perpetuating segregation. To keep the

pressure on, cooperating attorney Fred Noland prepared legal papers should the School Board fail to move. Negotiations with school officials progressed. Neither the School Board nor the general citizenry wanted to risk placing control of school policies in the hands of a judge. Finally in 1977 Superintendent David Moberly presented a comprehensive desegregation plan, including mandatory busing. After several months of intensive public discussion, the School Board adopted a plan by a 6-1 vote.

Thus, Seattle became the nation's largest metropolitan school district to desegregate without a court order. However, the battle over desegregation was not over. Organized groups of White parents had long resisted the notion of mandatory student transfers, some for racist reasons, others from a preference for neighborhood schools. In November of 1978 opponents of mandatory desegregation won passage of statewide Initiative 350, which required students to attend their neighborhood school. Busing for racial balance was not among the limited exemptions it allowed. The Seattle School District challenged the measure in court, with the ACLU-W as plaintiff's intervening party. U.S. District Court Judge Donald Voorhees declared Initiative 350 unconstitutional, in part for failing to recognize that a school district could have a constitutional duty to support racial busing even in the absence of a court order. In 1982 the U.S. Supreme Court affirmed the decision 5-4.

Stability

For its first three decades the ACLU-W had functioned as a mostly volunteer, shoestring operation. In the 1960s it had taken on its first full-time paid staff and had greatly increased its membership and budget. In the financial crunch of the 1970s the group continued with active programs but struggled to stay afloat. The lifting of the debt burden at the beginning of a new decade paved the way for further organizational development.

The first half of the 1980s saw increasing attacks on civil liberties. As did the John Birch Society crusades of the 1960s and the Watergate scandals of the 1970s, the threats of the Reagan era brought a flood of new members. With an aggressive recruitment campaign, the ACLU-W raised its membership by 60 percent, from 3,168 at the beginning of 1980 to 5,110 by the end of 1985.

In 1980, the year of Ronald Reagan's election as President, the ACLU-W hired Kathleen Taylor as executive director; she had previously worked with the group as coordinator of a series of police-community dialogues and of the Coalition on Government Spying. Taylor set a priority of achieving fiscal stability and making operations more professional. For years the ACLU-W's fundraising efforts had been crisis-oriented, and the resultant flow of income uncertain. Yet a veritable revolution had occurred in approaches to managing nonprofit organizations since the days of the Peter, Paul, and Mary concert. From the experiences of larger ACLU affiliates and the national office, the ACLU-W adopted more sophisticated techniques. It augmented the annual auction with a yearly Bill of Rights Calendar filled with pages sponsored by supporters. It instituted a Major Gifts Campaign to solicit large contributions from individual donors. The hiring of Joan O'Connor in 1983 as the group's first full-time fundraiser expressed this recognition that fundraising was an ongoing task.

The combination of increased membership, larger average contributions per member, and better fundraising brought in sums of money beyond the wildest dreams of the group's founders. The budget soared from $80,000 in 1981 to $282,000 in 1985, this time without going into the red. Back on its feet again, the ACLU-W could expand programs. In 1980 it made Julya Hampton full-time legal program director to oversee the growing docket and stable of cooperating attorneys. In 1982 it restored the legislative lobbyist position (lost to budgetary constraints in 1978), hiring Jerry Sheehan, who had served as Deputy Special Master for Judge Tanner in the Walla Walla prison case. By 1985 the staff had grown to seven full-time and two part-time positions.

In 1966 executive director Dave Guren had described the ACLU-W's evolution: "Our organizational character is changing of our own volition, from that of a small, loosely organized, poorly financed legal advocate to that of a larger, better organized, adequately financed, action-oriented educator and lobbyist." By the 1980s the transition from a network of friends and associates to an institution was complete.

Many longtime mainstays, such as Mary Gallwey, Alex Gottfried,

Fran Hoague, Art Kobler, and Ken MacDonald, remained active. And a new generation of leadership emerged, people whose formative experience was not McCarthyism but the Vietnam War; among them were Judy Bendich, Phil Bereano, Bob Beckerman, Peter Eglick, and Peter Greenfield. As a larger organization, the group's style changed. Not all board members knew each other, and the bonds of camaraderie were looser. The board and committees became more impersonal as the new members preferred meetings more task-oriented and tightly run. But concern for principles remained unchanged.

The Religious Right

The presence of a larger, stronger civil liberties organization was especially important in the 1980s because "the opposition" was increasingly well-financed and well-organized. The election of Ronald Reagan partly reflected the rising influence of fundamentalist religious groups. Mobilizing supporters via computer-targeted mass mailings, the religious right pressured politicians to roll back many civil liberties gains of the previous two decades. While Reagan's rhetoric talked of "getting the government off the backs of the people," in actuality his supporters often favored limiting personal freedom and intruding on privacy. Right-wing groups fervently called for banning abortion, restoring prayer to public schools, censoring books in libraries and schools, and overturning laws protecting gay rights.

A leading manifestation of the religious right in Washington was the Moral Majority, a national group founded by evangelist Jerry Falwell in 1979. Wrapping itself in a cloak of patriotism and righteousness, it injected the fundamentalist agenda into the political arena. Civil libertarians and other opponents countered with bumper stickers proclaiming "The Immoral Minority" and "The Moral Majority is Neither." ACLU-W board member Dan Levant debated Washington Moral Majority leader Michael Farris five times during 1981. At the same time the ACLU-W took pleasure in turning the other cheek to support the Moral Majority in a matter before the State Public Disclosure Commission. The Moral Majority had been ordered by the Commission to register as a political committee — a move which would have required release of its membership lists. The ACLU-W strongly protested the Commission's action and the Commission backed down.

Aggressive defense of civil liberties combined with Washington's generally tolerant social climate to prevent the often narrow-minded views of the Moral Majority from making much headway. The group waned as a political force by the mid-1980s, though some of the issues it had raised lingered. Seeking to improve its image, the Moral Majority rechristened itself the Bill of Rights Legal Foundation, an ironic choice of name, to be sure.

Public schools were a favorite forum for evangelical groups. In 1980 the ACLU-W established a Church-State Committee in response to a leap in the number of complaints about religious activities in the schools. In heavily publicized disputes in 1982 and 1983, pressure from the ACLU-W caused several school districts to cancel in-school assemblies featuring born-again members of the Seattle Seahawks, who sought to tell students how God had helped them cope with the pressures of professional sports. In 1984 the ACLU-W organized a coalition of 13 groups which submitted a Rulemaking Petition to the Superintendent of Public Instruction requesting

---

Freedom of Religion: The Hare Krishna Case

In 1970 a jeweler in Seattle's University District complained that saffron-robed members of the Hare Krishna sect were disturbing his customers by chanting in front of the nearby Varsity Theater. Police arrested three sect members under a city ordinance forbidding disturbing others by "yelling, shouting, chanting, hooting" and similar activities.

During a lengthy Municipal Court trial, the ACLU-W's Jan Peterson and Robert Welden presented theological explanations for each of the Hare Krishna chants. At one point a witness began chanting, and spectators in the courtroom followed suit. The judge turned a deaf ear to their plea and found the defendants guilty. However, King County Superior Court Judge Horton Smith reversed the conviction on grounds that the law had been applied unconstitutionally to interfere with the religious principles of people taught to go chanting in public.

statewide guidelines on religious activities in public schools. The State Board of Education responded by mandating that each local district issue its own set of rules. The action was a step toward clarifying policies but meant that infringements of the separation of church and state would have to be fought on a district-by-district basis.

Fears by fundamentalist parents that "secular humanism" was poisoning school reading materials sparked a series of heated conflicts. Small groups of parents set up "Education Information Councils" modelled after a successful censorship campaign run in Texas by Mel and Norma Gabler. They worked to purge texts of influences which, in their view, undermined religion, patriotism, parental authority, traditional sex roles, and the free enterprise system. In Renton a parents council in 1979 attacked the women's health book *Our Bodies, Our Selves*. Executive director Peter Judge and cooperating attorney Robert Alsdorf represented the ACLU-W at a meeting in which the school board voted 3-2 to keep the book as a library resource.

A parent in Mead School District in 1980 objected to a reading assignment of *The Learning Tree*, Gordon Parks's novel frankly portraying his boyhood as a Black in Kansas in the 1920s. The mother complained of the book's swear words, description of premarital sex, portrayals of violence, and blasphemies against Christ. When the School Board, upon investigation, ruled the book appropriate for a 10th-grade English class optional reading list, the parent, with the help of the Moral Majority, sued to have it removed from the curriculum. At the request of the school district the ACLU-W submitted an *amicus* brief defending the book's use. In 1982 Judge Robert McNichols of the Federal District Court in Spokane dismissed the *Grove v. Mead* suit. He ruled that there was no reason for the book to be thrown out and that constitutional rights had not been abridged since the student had been provided an alternate reading assignment. The Ninth Circuit Court of Appeals upheld the decision.

The battles were not just in the courtroom. The ACLU-W began organizing. Together with the Washington Booksellers Association and Washington Library Association, it formed the Washington Coalition Against Censorship, a statewide network of more than 20 groups willing to stand up to self-appointed censors.

Among its activities the group staged public readings from books that at one time or another have been banned. The ACLU-W also sponsored a School Censorship Project directed by Therese Ogle. Using the slogan "Empty Shelves, Empty Minds," the project helped the censorship coalition coordinate a statewide series of workshops to give parents, teachers, and librarians the tools to fight censorship. They explained that restricting reading material is an effort to eliminate diversity and free inquiry from schools and society at large.

One effect of censorship battles can be to create a generalized air of intimidation. For example, 33 books in the Evergreen School District were removed from a junior high library shelf without hearing or notice. The District's Instructional Media Committee approved the action even though no complaints had been filed by students, parents, or the citizenry. In 1983 the ACLU-W sued in Clark County Superior Court on behalf of district parents and students seeking return of the books. The district agreed to put back all but two. (The suit is still pending as of summer, 1987.)

Something Old, Something New

With the public mood growing more conservative, the 1980s reminded the ACLU of its founder Roger Baldwin's dictum, "No fight for civil liberties ever stays won." The decade saw old issues resurface and others emerge in new forms. Military conscription, which harked back to the ACLU's origins in World War I, again became a concern when President Jimmy Carter in 1980 announced renewal of registration for the draft. The ACLU nationally opposed the action as paving the way for a peacetime draft. The ACLU-W embarked on a statewide campaign to encourage lawful resistance to registration and to urge people to express their opposition. It helped staff information tables near registration sites at Post Offices and distributed "I Am Registering Under Protest" stickers to be put on registration forms.

Fighting intrusive searches became a major theme for the ACLU-W in the '80s. Many of the searches were directed at young people, a continuing target of government excess. When youthful rock music fans were subjected to patdown searches before concerts at Seattle Center (a city-owned facility), the ACLU responded. In 1980 ACLU-W cooperating attorneys Peter Eglick, Bob Beckerman, and Michael Gendler sued the City of Seattle on behalf of four concert-goers, asserting that searches without individualized suspicion violated Fourth Amendment and state constitutional protections against unreasonable search and seizure. One plaintiff had pills for a heart condition confiscated in a pre-concert search. In *Jacobsen et al. v. City of Seattle*, King County Superior Court Judge Terrence Carroll ruled the general searches unconstitutional, a decision the State Supreme Court upheld unanimously in 1983.

With *Jacobsen* the State Supreme Court began recognizing the special privacy protections provided by the Washington State Constitution. In 1982 school officials prevented Hazen High student Adam Kuehn from traveling to Canada with his school band when he refused to let them inspect his luggage in advance. The authorities wanted to search for alcohol, which had been a problem on earlier trips. A lower court judge ruled that the search was reasonable and raised no significant constitutional question. But in 1985 the State Supreme Court reversed this decision, agreeing with the ACLU's Michael Gendler and Harvey Grad that the Federal and state constitutions restrict searches unless there are reasonable

---

Joggers' Rights: The Stone Case

Luther Stone was jogging on the road near his Mountlake Terrace home at 5:30 one morning. Finding him breathing heavily and perspiring in an area where some vandalism had occurred, police stopped him and asked to see some ID. When Stone refused, he was charged with "obstructing a public officer" by failing to furnish "any statement, report or information lawfully required."

ACLU-W cooperating attorney John Bundy argued that the obstruction statute was too vague and that a citizen should not be required to show identification without probable cause to believe the person has committed or is about to commit a crime. Stone was convicted in Municipal Court, a decision upheld by Snohomish County Superior Court. In 1971 the Court of Appeals tossed out the conviction on grounds that the obstruction law was unconstitutionally vague.

grounds to believe a student is involved in illegal activity.

Other student rights conflicts also resurfaced. One highly publicized case involved Matthew Fraser, a Bethel High School senior who delivered a nominating speech on behalf of a student government candidate in 1983. Included were sexual double entendres, such as "I know a man who is firm" and ". . . a man who will go to the very end, even the climax, for each and every one of you." School authorities found the talk inappropriate and offensive. They imposed a three-day suspension on the senior and ruled that he would not be allowed to speak at graduation, an honor which fellow students had voted him.

ACLU-W cooperating attorney Jeff Haley argued in Federal District Court that Fraser's speech, while perhaps juvenile, had not been disruptive. Judge Jack Tanner agreed, concluding Fraser's talk was protected by the First Amendment since it wasn't obscene and did not disrupt the educational process. He ordered the suspension set aside and directed that Fraser be allowed to speak at graduation. The student's address centered on the right of free speech. The Ninth Circuit Court of Appeals upheld the decision, noting that school officials cannot use their own notion of appropriate speech to punish students. But in 1985 the U.S. Supreme Court reversed the lower courts. The turnaround created a new exception to freedom of speech by ruling that school officials have the right to regulate a talk at an assembly so as to teach students "appropriate" forms of expression.

Activists continued to run into problems in exercising free speech, too. In 1970 an ACLU-W member had been arrested in the parking lot of a Lynnwood roller rink for handing out leaflets announcing an ACLU meeting. Cooperating attorney Ron Meltzer had convinced the Snohomish County prosecutor to drop the charges. Ten years later an environmental group opposed to the WPPSS nuclear program sought to collect initiative petition signatures at Alderwood Mall in Lynnwood. The mall's owners brought suit, claiming that the First Amendment right to petition extended only to public, not private, property. ACLU-W cooperating attorney Rita Bender filed an *amicus* brief arguing that the Washington State Constitution's free speech protections covered the petitioners' actions. In 1981 the State Supreme Court backed the right of citizens to solicit initiative petition signatures in the common areas of the private mall. However, the ACLU-W would have to go to court repeatedly to have the right enforced for other groups at other malls.

The largest political demonstrations of the early 1980s were those opposing the nuclear arms race. To limit protest and attendant adverse publicity, the U.S. Coast Guard adopted sweeping rules limiting a planned nonviolent vigil marking the arrival of the first nuclear-armed Trident submarine to Puget Sound in 1982. ACLU-W cooperating attorneys Henry Aronson and Kelby Fletcher joined with the National Lawyers Guild to challenge the regulations. Federal District Court Judge Barbara Rothstein ordered the parties to reach an accommodation. The Coast Guard backed off somewhat to permit protest outside a 1,000-yard zone around the submarine. A nine-member ACLU-W observation team on a boat monitored the demonstration as a flotilla of small craft staged a dramatic confrontation with the mighty *U.S.S. Ohio*. The Coast Guard dealt with the "menace" of pacifists by shooting water cannons at their sailboats and reneging on part of the agreement by arresting protesters outside the 1,000-yard security zone; the pacifists were handcuffed and guarded with M-16s. All charges were dropped a week later.

The awesome power of nuclear weapons inevitably brought demands for government secrecy and restrictions on citizens' free speech rights. In 1984, after several years of consideration, the ACLU-W became the second affiliate to declare preparations for nuclear warfare a violation of civil liberties.

Overreaction by law enforcement officials had the ACLU-W again fighting searches. A Port Angeles woman held on traffic charges and a Renton woman arrested for making too much noise at a Halloween party were subjected to strip searches despite the minor nature of their offenses. ACLU-W cooperating attorneys Gene Chellis and Margaret McKeown sued to have the humiliating searches declared illegal unless there was reason to believe a weapon, contraband, or evidence was concealed. In 1983 both Clallam County and King County officials signed consent decrees ending indiscriminate strip searches. In the next two years, at the ACLU's insistence, the State Legislature passed laws requiring a warrant for body cavity searches, setting standards for the conduct of strip searches, and limiting their use against suspects of minor offenses.

A different form of invasion of privacy long opposed by the civil liberties group was the use of lie-detector tests on employees. In 1972, the ACLU-W had aided the Seattle Police Officers' Guild in fighting an attempt to force them to take lie-detector exams. In the early 1980s the conflict arose again when Michael Lloyd was suspended from his job as security officer at Seattle's Cabrini Hospital for refusing to take a polygraph test. Hospital administrators were conducting an investigation because $20 was missing from a coin purse left in the lost-and-found area. Given the choice of taking the test, resigning, or being fired, Lloyd, a mild-mannered man, chose to resign. He also called the ACLU-W, which took up his case. Washington state law prohibits an employer from requiring a lie-detector test as a condition for hiring or continued employment. Handled by Linda Cochran, the case was settled with Lloyd winning $25,000 in damages and Cabrini agreeing not to compel polygraph tests in the future. In 1985 the State Legislature passed an ACLU-sponsored bill strengthening the right of employees to sue for damages if they suffer for refusing to submit to examination by lie-detector.

As it entered its second 50 years, infringements of privacy presented the greatest challenges to the ACLU-W. Mandatory urinalysis tests for drugs, the threat of mandatory AIDS testing, electronic spying on workers on the job, the spread of computerized files on citizens' private lives — these are the frontier issues of liberties in the mid-1980s. Coping with them will require the same dedication that defenders of personal freedom have shown in the first 50 years of the ACLU-W.

Sources

Books

Vern Countryman, *Un-American Activities in Washington State: The Work of the Canwell Committee* (Ithaca, NY: Cornell University Press, 1951).

William Dwyer, *The Goldmark Case: An American Libel Trial* (Seattle: University of Washington Press, 1984).

Albert Gunns, *Civil Liberties in Crisis: The Pacific Northwest, 1917-1940* (NY: Garland Publishing, 1983).

Melvin Rader, *False Witness* (Seattle: University of Washington Press, 1969).

Jane Sanders, *Cold War on Campus* (Seattle: University of Washington Press, 1979).

ACLU Publications

ACLU (National) — *Annual Reports.*

Civil Liberties in Washington State, 1954-1959.

ACLU of Washington News, 1960-1970.

Civil Liberties, 1970-present.

ACLU-W "Legal Dockets."

(Newsletters available at ACLU-W offices — 1720 Smith Tower, Seattle, WA. 98104 and University of Washington, Suzzallo Library's Northwest Collection.)

Manuscript Collections

Available at University of Washington Historical Collections, University of Washington.

ACLU-W Archives.

Papers of individual ACLU members, including Phil Burton, Irving Clark, Mary Farquharson, Alex Gottfried, Austin Griffiths, Ed Henry, Adele Parker-Bennett, Solie Ringold, Len Schroeter, Ann Widditsch.

Interviews with ACLU Members

Arthur Barnett, John Caughlan, John Darrah, Hugh Fleetwood, Mary Gallwey, Aron Gilmartin, Alex Gottfried, Dave Guren, Ed Henry, Fran Hoague, Art Kobler, Ken Mac-Donald, Michael Rosen, Len Schroeter, Kathleen Taylor, Chris Young, Al Ziontz.

Miscellaneous

Fran and Betty Hoague, "The ACLU of Washington: A Short History," 1985.

Mason Morisset, "The American Civil Liberties Union of Washington: A Survey," 1965.

American Civil Liberties Union of Washington

Presidents		Executive Secretaries/ Executive Directors*	
1948	Donald Wollett	1948	Paul Parks (volunteer)
1949	John Richards	1951	Jack Harlow (volunteer)
1951-1953	Ed Munro		Max Nicolai (volunteer)
1953-1954	Kenneth MacDonald	1952	Nick Hughes (volunteer)
1955	Aron Gilmartin		R. Boland Brooks (first part-time paid)
1956	Francis Hoague	1953-1957	R. Boland Brooks
1957-1958	Melvin Rader		
1958	Robert Windsor	1958-1959	Hilde Applebaum
1959	Solie Ringold		
1960	Arval Morris	1960	Dave Smith
1961-1962	Melvin Rader	1961-1963	John Darrah
1963-1964	Leonard Schroeter	1964-1966	David Guren (first full-time director)
1965	John Sullivan		
1965-1966	Alvin Ziontz	1967	Henry Schroerluke (two months)
1967-1968	Arthur Kobler	1968	Len Mandelbaum
1969-1971	Hugh Fleetwood	1969-1971	Michael Rosen
1972-1973	Ann Widditsch	1972-1976	Lauren Selden
1974-1978	Mary Gallwey	1976-1978	David Harrison
1979-1981	Kay Frank	1979	Peter Thomas Judge
1981-1983	Judy Bendich	1980-	Kathleen Taylor
1984-	Peter Eglick		

* Until 1961 these people were considered secretaries rather than executive directors.